# BeautyQueens

Candace Savage

A PLAYFUL HISTORY

# BeautyQueens

ABBEVILLE PRESS PUBLISHERS

NEW YORK LONDON PARIS

*Dressed for success in bathing suits and high heels, women from more than two dozen countries pose for the official photographer of the Miss Universe beauty pageant in 1956.* Albert R. Kelch, Archives of the Historical Society of Long Beach

*Previous page: With their fingers crossed for luck, six bright-eyed beauties gaze at the crown that one of them will wear as Miss Rheingold for 1956. The competition (held throughout the 1940s and 1950s) was sponsored by a brewery, with the winner chosen by public balloting. In 1951, the race to "rule beerdom" became the second-largest election in the United States, with 25 million votes counted.* Al Ravenna, *New York World-Telegram and Sun,* Library of Congress

Text copyright © 1998 by Candace Savage. Photographs copyright © 1998 as credited. All rights reserved under international copyright conventions. No part of this book may be reproduced or utilized in any form or by any means, electronic or mechanical, including photocopying, recording, or by any information storage and retrieval system, without permission in writing from the publisher. Inquiries should be addressed to Abbeville Publishing Group, 22 Cortlandt Street, New York, N.Y. 10007. The text of this book was set in Perpetua. Printed and bound in Hong Kong.

First edition
10 9 8 7 6 5 4 3 2 1

*Library of Congress Cataloging-in-Publication Data*
Savage, Candace Sherk, 1949–
    Beauty queens : a curious history / Candace Savage.
        p.   cm.
    Includes bibliographical references and index.
    ISBN 0-7892-0492-4
    1. Beauty contests--United States.      2. Feminine beauty
(Aesthetics)--United States.    I. Title.
HQ1220.U5S26     1998
791.6--dc21                      98-4378

Every attempt has been made to trace accurate ownership of copyrighted visual material in this book. Errors and omissions will be corrected in subsequent editions, provided notification is sent to the publisher.

The verse from "French Heels" on page viii is reprinted by permission of Jay Livingstone Music, Inc., MCA Music Publishing Co., on behalf of St. Angelo Music.

The Canada Council provided the author with a short-term grant to support the completion of this book.

Front cover photograph: Unidentified postcard, 1950s
Back cover photograph: Princeton Antiques, Atlantic City
Design by Barbara Hodgson

# Contents

The New Crop of Peac
SANTA ROSA, CALIF

# Confessions
## of an Armchair Beauty

When I was eleven or twelve in the early 1960s, my loving and ruthless mother offered me an unsparing assessment of my prospects in life. It was a good thing I had brains, she said, looking me up and down, because I was highly unlikely to get very far on my appearance alone. My dad amplified this assessment one day by telling me that I was "built like a battleship," a remark he intended me to accept as a compliment. But as he could no doubt tell from the wry face I pulled, this was not a phrase that the average young girl was dying to hear.

Inexperienced though I was in affairs of the heart, I was well versed in the language of love, and words like "brains" and "battleship" were not in the lexicon. The pink-bound teen romances that I borrowed by the armload from the public library studiously avoided any reference to female intelligence and instead did a brisk trade in adjectives like "pert," "bouncy," "tender" and "glowing." What's more, no romance heroine would ever have been likened to a piece of military hardware, however admiringly. Her qualities were more ethereal by far and could best be associated with wonders of the natural world such as sunsets, bird song and soft summer winds. "My dear," the handsome hero would whisper, as he stroked his girl's downy cheek, "you have the grace of a slender willow tree." Would anyone ever say such dreamy things to me?

*An old French maxim says it all:* Il faut souffrir pour être belle. *[One must suffer to be beautiful.] This is me, about age 13.* Harry Sherk

*Facing page: Their faces alight with perkiness and good cheer, these "peaches" from the beaches of California probably date from the 1930s.*

*All day long in my sloppy jeans*
*I just romp like a pup.*
*But at night I put my French*
*Heels on*
*And a teen-age girl grows up.*

—"French Heels," sung by Debbie Reynolds,

about 1960

At that time, I had to admit it didn't seem very likely. Although I might be clever and strong, in my mom's and dad's eyes at least, it was obvious to all concerned that I was no beauty. If the small prairie town where I lived had had a soda fountain (which it did not), I would clearly have run no risk of being "discovered" by a talent scout and whisked off to Hollywood. No matter how I primped and posed and slathered on mascara, I simply could not make myself look like Debbie Reynolds. The reigning teen queen of the day, Miss Reynolds (a former Miss Burbank) was svelte, fine featured and perky, like the girls in the romance books. I was short and plump, with big front teeth, bushy eyebrows and stubborn, straight-as-string hair. What's more, my mother said I had a smart mouth, and there was nothing pretty, she assured me, about a lippy girl.

Beauty was like baseball: I was just no good at it. But that didn't exempt me from playing the game or keep me from dreaming that, just once, I'd step up to the plate with the bases loaded and hit a grand slam. When it came to the sport of beauty, I didn't set my sights too high. I never aspired to be queen of the fall fair or the Valentine's dance. (Frankly, I wasn't prepared to be *nice* long enough to attain anything so grand.) But what I did want—what I longed for, with a hopeless, sickly teenage desire—was the admiring attention of a small, handpicked selection of boys. Boys like Tim in grade eight, who shocked everyone by claiming that he wanted to be a *Playboy* photographer; or Steve in grade ten, whose mother, notoriously, was having an affair with an appliance dealer; or someone called "R.S.," whose name I no longer recall but whose initials are still inscribed, with furtive passion, inside my desk drawer.

Does he love me? love me not? Would he like me better if I wore more eye shadow? less? If I wedged my stocky body into a panty girdle? If I lost five pounds or ten? If I smiled and giggled and flirted with him after French class? And what did I think of *myself* when, as my teen years progressed, I invented and reinvented my image through the feminine artifices of makeup, hairpieces, hair removal, high heels, body toning, calisthenics, corsetry and studied cuteness?

"All day long in my sloppy jeans, I just romp like a pup. But at night I put my French Heels on, and a teen-age girl grows up. Doo-wah-wah." As pathetic as it now seems, Debbie Reynolds's hit song "French Heels" was the anthem of my dawning maturity.

Compared with the round-the-clock influence of girls' fiction and pop tunes, beauty contests made only an occasional—if nonetheless indelible—impression on my teenage definition of womanhood. By the time my family got its first TV, circa 1964, the Miss America Pageant had been beaming its message into millions of homes for a decade, and the Miss Canada competition was already into its second year on CTV. Although I would have been well into my teens at the time, my first TV pageant has not left a detailed trace in my mind. All that remains is a hazy sense of a screen filled to bursting with romance heroines. Girls with unromantic addresses in Prince George, British Columbia, and Pine Bluff, Arkansas, floated in front of the cameras amid billows of chiffon. To the cynic in me, they looked like a fleet of animated lamp-shades or vivified meringues.

It was all very silly, and I knew it even then. The romance stories I fed myself on were trashy and cheap, with cardboard characters, stock plots and treacly endings. Smart aleck that I was, I mocked them as "and-he-kissed-her" books because of the inevitable, climacteric moment when the good-girl heroine got her man. But this ele-vated analysis did nothing to temper my compulsive desire for happy endings, and my loud-mouthed scorn of beauty contests did not prevent me from watching the tele-casts to their glitzy and glorious conclusions. Yes, the girls looked ridiculous as they swanned their beehived heads; yes, the interview questions and answers made me squirm with embarrassment. The bathing-suit judging was tacky, and the "talent" per-formances made Ed Sullivan's weekly lineup look like a night at the Met. But the crowning of the winner—so "natural, young and sweet"—sent an electric thrill of pleasure through my pubescent body.

Dream the impossible dream: let it be me, let it be me . . .

Beauty contests on TV were a magic mirror that, willy-nilly, made every girl and woman into a participant, whether she was built like a willow or like a fortress; and recalcitrant tomboys like me were not exempt. In our dizzy identification with win-ners and losers alike, a whole generation of women and girls in the fifties and sixties tumbled in a narcissistic dream of our own potential perfection. I know, because I was one of them. Against my better judgment and with my whole heart, I was an arm-chair beauty contestant. And then, one day in 1968, the world began to improve—not only for brains and battleships but for beauties, too.

*Overleaf: In the twenties, beauty contests were sometimes used to promote a virile and well-muscled vision of female loveliness. In 1927, for example, a bevy of broad-shouldered beauties took the stage at the Capital Theatre in Edmonton, Alberta. Sadly for me, no hint of this ideal remained by the 1960s. McDermid, Glenbow Archives, ND-3-3471*

*It is better to be looked over than overlooked.*

—Mae West, *Belle of the Nineties*, 1934

# Miss Steak

On September 7, 1968, a pretty, spirited young woman from Belvidere, Illinois, wiped away the obligatory tears of joy as she was crowned Miss America for 1969. Her name was Judi Ford and, despite her meticulously penciled-in eyebrows, spunsugar hair and permanent smile, she was not a stereotypically spineless and sappy beauty contestant. "I was eighteen, that's all," she later recalled, "and a kid-around person." She was also refreshingly stubborn. When her advisers had tried to persuade her to dye her hair brown (on the grounds that all the winners for ten years had been brunettes), she refused to make the change. A blonde she had been born, and a blonde she would remain. Called upon to demonstrate her "talent" as part of the contest, she had bypassed the usual amateur musical renditions—the warbled arias, the thunderous concertos—and instead had performed gymnastic stunts on her trampoline. Most disturbing of all to her handlers, she smoked cigarettes, though surreptitiously since becoming a beauty contestant.

"Everywhere you go, everyone you meet, they think of Miss America as being extra-sweet," Judi Ford quickly noticed; so everywhere she went, she did her best to contradict this impression by acting as much as she could like her own irrepressible self. For this she no doubt deserves her own brief footnote in the annals of women's liberation, but she is not likely to get it. For on that same day in the fall of 1968, outside the Convention Hall in Atlantic City where she was crowned, another coronation

*When New York Radical Women took their protest to the streets of Atlantic City in the fall of 1968, their membership increased fivefold within a week.* AP/Wide World Photos

*Facing page: Moments before a New York beauty contest, a team of attendants puts the finishing touches on their "girl." (Nowadays, a quick blast of spray adhesive would be used to keep the bathing suit in place.)*

*In addition to being judged in swimwear, this contestant will likely undergo an evening-gown competition, personal and onstage interviews, and perhaps a talent show.* Walter Kaner Associates, *New York World-Telegram and Sun,* Library of Congress

took place, one that through its sheer outrageousness pushed the teenaged struggles of Judi Ford onto the back page. Shortly after noon, a group of singing, slogan-chanting women—one or two hundred strong—established themselves with their megaphones and placards on the Boardwalk. There, under the watchful eye of the police and in full view of the media that had gathered to photograph Miss Ford's moment of glory, the protesters ceremonially crowned their own beauty winner. With careful disregard for subtlety, they bestowed the title of Miss America on a sheep.

Although the organizers proudly announced that women had come from as far away as Florida, Michigan and Canada to join the protest, the action had actually been conceived by a small "underground" group known to themselves (and to almost no one else) as New York Radical Women. As radicals, the members of NYRW had all previously been active in civil-rights and New Left organizations; as women, they had all been stung by the gross sexism that prevailed in sixties' revolutionary circles. Which of them had not seethed as some self-important male leader assigned all the serious decisions to himself and then called for "chicks to volunteer for cooking duty"? Which one had not smarted from activist Stokely Carmichael's notorious pronouncement that the proper position for women in civil-rights work was "prone"?

It didn't take long for "the girls in the movement" (in *Time* magazine's memorable phrase) to figure out that their leaders were "possibly less interested in women's rights" than were their archenemies, including soon-to-be president Richard Nixon. If men of every political stripe were the problem, it followed that women themselves were the answer. "We must provide a place for women to be friends, exchange personal griefs, and give their sisters moral support—in short develop group consciousness," read one early Women's Liberation manifesto, circa 1967. Among the first groups to put this revolutionary premise to work was New York Radical Women, formed early the following year, just a few months before they and their beribboned sheep came into public view.

With a membership that included intellectual street fighters like Robin Morgan and Shulamith Firestone, NYRW was determined to become a "political force to be reckoned with." "Power only cooperates with power," Firestone observed, and women could only achieve influence from a position of strength. Yet femininity, by its very definition, implied weakness and political impotence. If women hoped to end racial

---

*The women who are parading around in there are being displayed to someone else's glory and profit. You note their sashes do not say "Ms. Jane Doe," but Miss Fresno, Miss Huntington Beach. They are displayed as exemplary products of the economy of their home towns.*

—D. A. Clarke, speech at the "Myth California"

protest, 1983

segregation—if they wanted to halt the rain of napalm over Vietnam—they could not approach the powers that be as passive supplicants. It was time for women to get tough.

In keeping with this belief, NYRW's first action had been a mock funeral for "Traditional Womanhood," which they had staged in Arlington Cemetery that January. Under a huge banner that read "DON'T CRY: RESIST," they carried the funeral bier of a large, blank-faced dummy with blonde curls and ultrafeminine attire. Hanging from the rigging were womanly accoutrements such as curlers, garters, hair spray and welfare stamps. It was with this demonstration still vivid in their minds that, a few months afterward, the group set its sights on the Miss America Pageant.

As Robin Morgan explained at the time, the women targeted the pageant after a thoroughgoing analysis. First and foremost, they objected to the event as "patently degrading to women." Far from representing the nation's ideal girl, Miss America was nothing but a "Mindless-Boob-Girlie Symbol" and a walking billboard for the "ludicrous 'beauty' standards that enslaved all women." What was perhaps even worse, these beauty standards were also racist. As of 1968, no African-American woman had ever taken her place among the finalists, much less carried the winner's bouquet. What's more, the winner and her runners-up were shipped off to Vietnam, where they entertained the troops and served, the protesters charged, as "death mascots" to an immoral war. And finally, for all the contest's lofty talk about honoring womanhood, its underlying purpose was simply, crassly, to sell its sponsors' products. The whole million-dollar enterprise was, Morgan proclaimed, nothing but a blatant "commercial shill-game." "Where else," she asked, "could one find such a perfect combination of American values—racism, militarism, capitalism—all packaged in one 'ideal' symbol, a woman?"

"This was, of course, the basic reason why the protesters disrupted the pageant—the contestants epitomize the role all women are forced to play in this society, one way or the other: apolitical, unoffending, passive, delicate (but drudgery-delighted) *things*."

But there was another reason, just as basic, for the decision to hit the Miss America contest. The pageant was a media magnet, one that, in the late sixties, still attracted the attention of every major newspaper on the continent. The annual telecast was one of the highest-rated programs of the year, garnering nearly two-thirds of the night's viewers. To capitalize on this huge audience, the protesters on the Boardwalk played

*This young Toronto woman braved the January cold to state her objection to the crowning of Miss Winter Bikini '69. Nearby, the grinning winner peeled back her fur coat to give photographers a glimpse of her gooseflesh.* Reed, *Toronto Telegram*, York University Archives

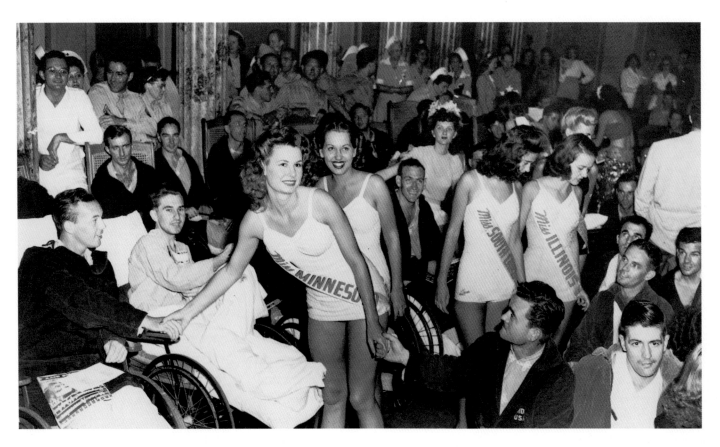

## The Living Bra and the Dead Soldier.
## We refuse to be used as
## Mascots for Murder.

—Feminist manifesto, 1968

The whole point of a beauty contest, in the protesters' critical view, was to find a girl who would "sell" to the public. She could then be used to market anything from underwear (as in the Bali brassiere promotion, left) to the national war effort. Here Patricia Ann Cummings, Billie Owens and Betty June King (representing Minnesota, South Carolina and Illinois respectively) visit with wounded soldiers in an Atlantic City hospital in 1944. Bert Nevins, Inc., *New York World-Telegram and Sun*, Library of Congress; AP/Historical Society of Pennsylvania

*A protester waves a bra aloft before consigning it to the Freedom Trash Can on the Boardwalk in Atlantic City.* AP/Wide World Photos

*Facing page: A woman is only a woman, but a donut is a snack. (Lu Anne Warren was a candidate for National Donut Week Queen in 1956.)* Photofest/Icon

to the media by singing, dancing and waving their slogans aloft. "No More Beauty Standards—Everyone is Beautiful." "Girls Crowned—Boys Killed." "Miss America is Alive and Angry—in Harlem." "Welcome to the Miss America Cattle Auction." The centerpiece of the ruckus was a large "Freedom Trash Can" into which the demonstrators tossed items of "woman-garbage," such as dish detergent, steno pads, false eyelashes, wigs, curlers and copies of *Cosmo, Ladies Home Journal* and *Playboy.* One woman, sixty-eight-year-old Mrs. Clara DeMiha, threw in her high heels amid cries of "Down with bound feet!" and "Tell it like it is!" Another brandished a girdle overhead, chanting "No more girdles, no more pain. No more trying to hold the fat in vain." Some even tossed in their brassieres—typical sixties' devices that looked more like effects from a science-fiction film than feminine undergarments.

All in all, as one participant (black activist and lawyer Flo Kennedy) put it, it was "the best fun I can imagine anyone wanting to have on any single day of her life." But the day was not pure sport. The protesters were ardent about their critique of the pageant, their insistence on speaking only to female reporters (who, in the sixties, were ordinarily confined to the women's pages), and their plan, if things got rough, "to reject all male authority and demand to be busted by policewomen only." ("In Atlantic City," as a preprotest press release gleefully pointed out, "women cops are not permitted to make arrests—dig that!") And, in fact, arrests *were* made—though by males, of course—when sixteen of the protesters took seats inside the Convention Hall during the telecast. One of them, Peggy Dobbins, a member of NYRW, was charged with "emanating a noxious odor" for spraying Toni home-permanent spray near the mayor's box. Several others were nabbed after a bedsheet-sized banner fluttered down over the audience. It bore just two words—WOMEN'S LIBERATION.

In the days and weeks after the pageant, those words rang round the globe. As Robin Morgan exulted afterward, the demonstration had announced the existence of Women's Lib to the world and drawn a host of eager adherents to the cause. To Morgan, the protest marked nothing less than the birth of the modern feminist movement.

SIZE OF THE DONUT HOLE
DOWN THROUGH THE YEARS
1936 - 1946 - 1956

1½"          7/8"          3/8"

[Pageants are degrading to women,] no matter how the promoters protest. . . . [But] I must admit that these contests hold a morbid fascination for me and I watch them all.

—Susan Brownmiller, 1983

And the women's revolution had begun in, of all the unlikely spots, "super tacky Atlantic City," at a beauty pageant.

Despite the protesters' success at getting their message out, there were aspects of their action that they later came to regret. One was the whole business of brassieres. At some time during the planning stages, someone had proposed ceremonially burning a bra, as a feminine equivalent to the burning of draft cards (a frequent gesture of dissent in antiwar protests). But when it came down to events, the bra burning did not occur due to lack of a fire permit. The newspapers, undeterred by the limitations of fact, went right ahead with their incendiary headlines. The protesters thus went down in history as bra burners, as if their whole purpose had been—as one pageant official put it—"to make women seem less attractive" by burning their undergarments.

If the trivialization of their message by outsiders was annoying, the organizers found their own errors of analysis more worrying. "We take the woman's side in everything," New York Radical Women had proclaimed in its statement of founding principles. "We take as our source the hitherto unrecognized culture of women, a culture which from long experience of oppression developed an intense appreciation for life, a sensitivity to . . . the complexity of simple things, [and] a powerful knowledge of human needs and feelings." Yet in carrying out their action, they had not acknowledged the complexity of their own feelings about the Miss America Pageant, an event that many of the group admitted was on their personal must-watch list. Others, like NYRW's Carol Hanisch, remembered identifying with the contest and weeping tears of joy with successive winners. Despite herself, and with her whole heart, she too had been an armchair participant.

The feminists' biggest mistake, in Hanisch's view, was to deny their own involvement in the cult of beauty. This omission had introduced a "definite strain of antiwomanism" into their action. "Posters which read 'Up Against the Wall, Miss America,' 'Miss America Sells It,' and 'Miss America is a Big Falsie' hardly raised any woman's consciousness and really harmed the cause of sisterhood," she concluded sadly. "Miss America and all beautiful women came off as our enemy instead of as our sisters who suffer with us." The whole subject was so touchy, so subtle, so unexpectedly complex. Yet the protesters had had no way to know in advance that by targeting beauty

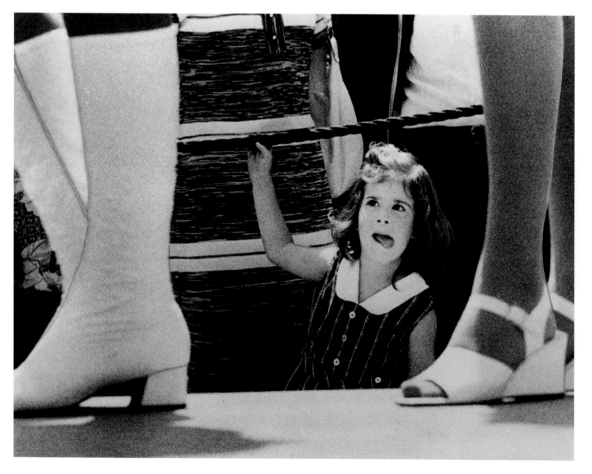

*Beauty contests put the everyday practices of femininity—dieting, shaving, tweezing, make-up and all the rest—on center stage, where they could be studied, imitated and critiqued by all interested parties. In the late sixties and early seventies, pageants attracted the attention of virtually everybody, including young Jennifer Hellen, seen here scrutinizing the lineup at the Miss Toronto competition in 1971.* Norm Betts, *Toronto Telegram,* York University Archives

pageants, they had blundered onto a cultural battlefield. For more than a century, beauty contests had provided a space in which competing definitions of womanhood were put in dispute and on display. When women (like the protesters) had allegiances in both camps, life could be expected to get a little tense.

In everyday life, these anxieties became minutely personal, as individual women debated whether or not to shave their armpits, wear bras or tune in to their favorite beauty pageants on television. But these decisions, so trivial in themselves, were signs and symptoms of a larger historical process. If the personal was political, as the feminists taught, then the discomforts of the present had their roots in the past.

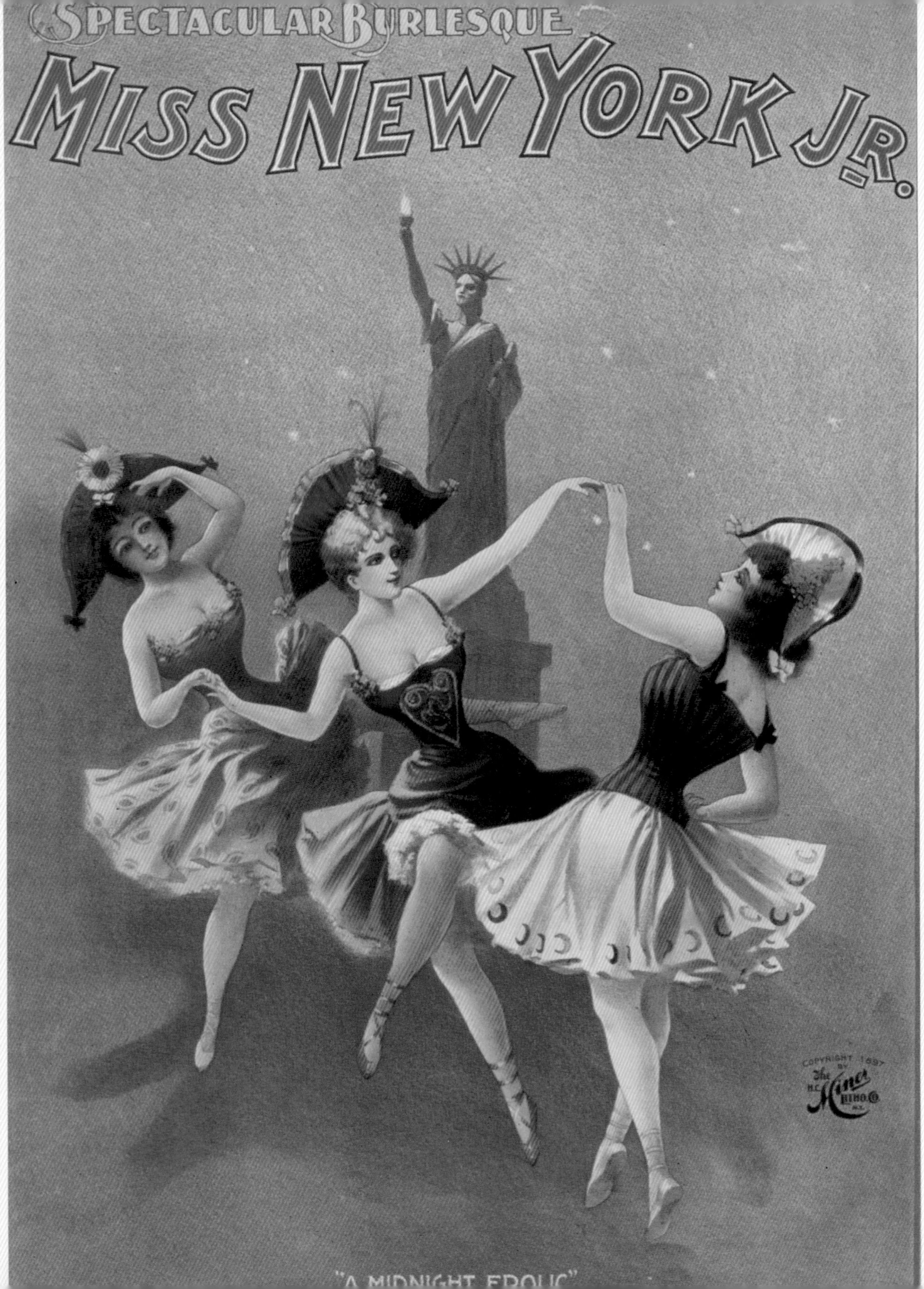
SPECTACULAR BURLESQUE
MISS NEW YORK JR.
COPYRIGHT 1897 BY
"A MIDNIGHT FROLIC"

# Heavy the Head
## That Wears the Crown

Whether or not one accepts the feminist critique of beauty pageants, judging women on their physical charms is surely a little crass. So it is not surprising that through the years contest promoters have attempted to dignify their efforts in whatever way they can. One favorite ploy has been to claim the prestige of classical origins. Beauty contests, it is said, first arose in ancient Greece and were duly memorialized in the famous case of the "judgment of Paris." According to legend, poor Paris—mere mortal though he was—had been called upon to settle a scrap among the goddesses. Who was the loveliest of all: Juno, Venus or Minerva? Who deserved to receive the golden apple marked "For the fairest"? By selecting Venus (and accepting Helen of Troy as a bribe), he settled the beauty conflict (and inadvertently ignited the Trojan War). Surely this made Venus the first Miss Olympus and Paris the first man to judge a beauty contest.

While it is true that the ancient Greeks prized beauty in women *and* men, there is no evidence that they held actual competitions. In cold point of fact, the spiritual father of the beauty contest was not a Greek hero but the consummate American showman Phineas T. Barnum (later of circus fame). In the early 1850s, Barnum was the proprietor of a "dime museum" in New York where, according to one contemporary assessment, he exercised his profound understanding of modern democracy. "He knew

*Ever on the lookout for subjects that afforded a voluptuous expanse of female flesh, Peter Paul Rubens produced several versions of* The Judgment of Paris, *including this one from 1600.* Reproduced by courtesy of the Trustees, the National Gallery, London

*Facing page: The showgirls of the New York theater were so French, so daring, so naughty—and so very popular at the turn of the century. What once might have been seen as pornography was now offered to the public as "harmless" entertainment. This liberalization of public taste paved the way for the first beauty contests, which also inherited the "lineup" formation from the burlesque.* Library of Congress LC-USZC2-426

By 1915, the annual baby parade at Asbury Park, New Jersey, was already established as one of the leading attractions on the New England coast. In the twenties and thirties, baby contests would be taken up by the eugenics movement as a means of encouraging "quality" breeding. Library of Congress LC-USZ62-98785

By the 1950s, beauty contests were a "normal" part of a little girl's summer fun. In Sanlando Springs, Florida, in 1956, "the tiny tots paraded and performed under adult rules" for the title of Little Miss Seven. In the end, talent-winner Jane Evans took second place to the well-turned-out Sharon Berry. UPI/ New York World-Telegram and Sun, Library of Congress

that 'the people' means crowds, paying crowds; that crowds love the fashion and will follow it; and that the business of a great man is to make and control the fashion." The fashion in commercial entertainment, as this great man saw it, was the merchandising of sensational curiosities—from "educated dogs" to human "novelties" —under the banner of art and learning. With some 600,000 items on display, the museum could claim to offer a little bit of "everything worth seeing and knowing." But of all its attractions, none were more popular than the contests Barnum occasionally sponsored. Dogs, birds, flowers, even children were displayed and judged for the pleasure of large, paying audiences. Almost 61,000 patrons swarmed his baby show in 1855, and multitudes were turned away at the door.

*At a Brooklyn playground in 1951, the judges wisely concluded that all of the contestants deserved to be winners.* Walter Albertin, New York World-Telegram and Sun, Library of Congress

A similar promotion the year before had been disappointing. Barnum had proposed to select and exhibit "the Handsomest Ladies" in America and the Canadas. But

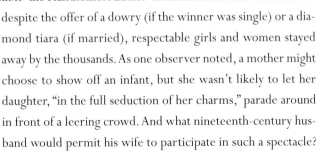

The dignity of woman consists in being unknown to the world. Her glory is the esteem of her husband; her pleasure the happiness of her family.

—philosopher Jean-Jacques Rousseau, eighteenth century

despite the offer of a dowry (if the winner was single) or a diamond tiara (if married), respectable girls and women stayed away by the thousands. As one observer noted, a mother might choose to show off an infant, but she wasn't likely to let her daughter, "in the full seduction of her charms," parade around in front of a leering crowd. And what nineteenth-century husband would permit his wife to participate in such a spectacle?

Undaunted by this reaction, Barnum announced an alternate plan. Entries for the contest would now be accepted in the form of photographic likenesses, and submissions from "disreputable persons" were formally banned. The photos would be displayed at his museum, and the hundred women who received the most votes from visitors would be honored with specially commissioned oil portraits. A select few of these paintings would then be reproduced in the forthcoming *World's Book of Female Beauty,* to be published in France. The whole

As nightly produced at LALLA ROOKH'S WELCOME. FOREPAUGH'S NEW OLYMPIA.

project, Barnum said, would serve the loftiest possible aims, *viz.* to "encourage a more popular taste for the Fine Arts, stimulate to extra exertion the genius of our Painters, and laudably gratify the public curiosity."

Although Barnum sold his museum before he could bring this scheme to fruition, his daring combination of lowbrow entertainment, highbrow culture and modern technology (the daguerreotype) set a pattern that would attract dozens of imitators in succeeding decades. In 1881, for example, more than eleven thousand women were persuaded to submit their likenesses to a contest organized by Barnum's chief circus rival, Adam Forepaugh, who offered his winner a whopping ten thousand dollars and the chance to star as the scantily clad temptress Lalla Rookh in a dramatization of an arty, erotic epic by poet Thomas Moore. The preordained winner, a bosomy actress named Louise Montague, was hired on condition that she forgo the cash award. Nonetheless, as "The $10,000 Beauty" and headline attraction of "The Mammoth Aggregation of Quintuplexal Wonders," she helped Forepaugh bring in the unheard-of sum of half a million dollars in two short seasons.

MISS LOUISE MONTAGUE.

*Touted far and wide as the $10,000 Beauty, Louise Montague received a weekly stipend of $100 for appearing as Lalla Rookh. "I only took the position for the excitement," she told the press in 1881. Claiming that the "legitimate theater" was her real forte, she expressed an intention to form her own theater troupe—or else to marry somebody with lots of cash.* Poster: Circus World Museum, Baraboo, Wisconsin; portrait: Hertzberg Circus Museum, San Antonio, Texas

*Facing page: When Barnum proposed his beauty contest in 1854, he hoped to appeal not only to female vanity but also to national pride. The "old countries" of Europe each laid claim to its own distinctive "type" of beauty as an emblem of national identity. Young countries like the United States, Australia and Canada, with their mixed population of immigrants, aspired to do the same.* Canadian Illustrated News, 1874, National Library of Canada

DAILY MIRROR BEAUTY CONTEST.
(IST. PRIZE WINNER)

*Miriam Babbage*

*In the early twentieth century, beauty contests were used as promotional gimmicks by newspapers and magazines in Canada, the United States, England, France and Australia, among other places. The postcard announcing the winner of London's* Daily Mirror *contest provides few details, though it appears to date from the time of the First World War. Mrs. C. A. Hunt of New South Wales (right) entered her photo in the World's Beauty Challenge of 1908—a contest organized by an Australian magazine in answer to a challenge from the* Chicago Tribune. National Library of Australia

Receipts of this magnitude could not have gone unnoticed by the newspapers that covered Forepaugh's progress across the United States. By the end of the decade, big-city dailies were sponsoring contests of their own in an attempt to increase circulation and boost their own profits. Nothing sells papers like pictures of pretty girls (a marketing truism that has held for more than a hundred years). In the course of one contest in 1905, newspaper editors in twelve cities were said to have scrutinized forty thousand photos in their search for the loveliest woman in the United States.

The laurels were ultimately awarded to Della Carson of Chicago, whose qualifications included a sweet-natured face and ultrarespectable employment at a local seminary.

By publishing photos of Miss Carson and other pleasing young women, newspapermen (like Barnum before them) pointed to their high-minded intentions. As the *New York Times* put it in 1907, photographic portraits were published as evidence that "the portrayal of types of feminine beauty is within the province of the camera artist as well as those who wield the brush and pencil." Although the old guard of nineteenth-century painters (in America and abroad) had busied themselves recording landscapes and historical events, the younger generation, largely schooled in France, fixed their eyes almost exclusively on the female form. Woman, naked or clothed, was the only subject deemed worthy of notice by any serious artist.

This was not a sign that the art world (which was dominated by men) had developed a sudden interest in the experiences and aspirations of the "gentle sex." Instead, it marked an awareness that women, like art and artists themselves, were presumed to exist on a higher plane than the crass, utilitarian culture surrounding them. By picturing women, painters were also representing their claim to a separate sphere for their art, in which abiding spiritual values outweighed the almighty dollar. The personal lives of the women they painted were therefore of no interest. What mattered was the opportunity to express one's artistic vision through explorations of pure form (as in Whistler's well-known *Arrangement in Grey and Black No. 1: The Artist's Mother*) or through allegorical presentations of worthy concepts—justice, science, the uses of wealth or the progress of civilization—all of which were pictured as female in turn-of-the-century works.

Again, it was not that actual women had, or should have had, any practical involvement with learning or economic power. "Real women" were above all these things, and it was because of their detachment from the dirty work of the world that they could so readily be abstracted as its symbols. A portrait of a man was inevitably overwritten with grubby distinctions from everyday life. Was he a tradesman or a tycoon? Did he vote Democrat or Republican, Liberal or Conservative? A picture of a woman, by contrast, was easily stripped of its individuality. A woman was just a woman—a blank canvas that could be inscribed with any number of predetermined meanings.

*Overleaf: Taking their inspiration from the art critic John Ruskin, many communities organized spring festivals that involved crowning the "likeablest and loveablest" of maidens. Cork, in Eire, had its Rose Queen (left), while in Washington, D.C., a May Queen (Irma Sweeny) was crowned by Spring (Dorothy Zimmerman).* Roehampton Institute, London; National Photo Collection, Library of Congress

The [pure young] girl is placed upon a pedestal and each

offers worship according to his abilities, the artist among the rest.

—*Critic Samuel Isham, 1905*

This was true whether she was a model in the studio or a "beauty" on page three of the local daily.

As the pure-souled devotees of ideal beauty, artists and art lovers defined their interests as wholly aesthetic. In any other context, gazing at women's bodies—peering, as it were, through the keyhole of the bathhouse or harem—might have seemed better suited to the peep shows in the Bowery. But in the rarefied realm of art, contemplating the female form was deemed to provide only refined, intellectual pleasures. Artists, by their calling, were freed from the base, sexual nature of other men. So when a model leaped out of a pie at an artists' stag party, her performance was legitimized by the character of her audience—"all socially and artistically of the best set," according to one of the painters who was present. Rather than being seen as a sex object to be ogled by dirty old men, the girl-in-the-pie had been transformed into an *objet d'art*.

Over in Britain, the eminent art critic and historian John Ruskin looked at women with the same kind of double vision. Deeply aggrieved by the ugliness of industrial cities, Ruskin yearned for the bygone pleasures of village life where, as he imagined it, peasants had taken delight in honest toil and simple people had wreathed their days in beauty and ritual. If only one could introduce a remembrance of this golden past into modern times! One possibility, he thought, would be to sponsor a revival of May Day and the May Queen. In its origins, the May festival seems to have been a fertility rite that was marked by the crowning of a queen *and* king and by sending the young folk into the woods for a night of revelry. ("I have heard it credibly reported . . . by men of great gravities and reputation," Phillip Stubbes lamented in 1583, "that of . . . a hundred maides going to the wood overnight, there have scaresly the third part of them returned home againe undefiled.") For obvious reasons, the celebration was suppressed by the Puritans in both Britain and the United States during the seventeenth century.

In promoting the revival of a May Queen festival, Ruskin was not endorsing a sexual free-for-all. In fact, sexual expression of any sort was one of his sore spots. His marriage of six years had ended unconsummated and, though he drooled over almost every female he met, his urges were invariably unassuaged. His particular passion was for young girls, whom he imagined to be as innocent and pure as his own admiration

Admiring the Beauty.

for them. The May Day celebration appealed to him not only as a vehicle for beautifying modern life but also as a comfort for Victorian males with deeply conflicted desires. Under Ruskin's sponsorship, a May Queen festival was established in 1881 at Whitelands, a women's college near London, and from there the custom quickly spread throughout England, Canada and the United States, as a pretty springtime ritual for schoolgirls.

The late nineteenth century loved its "traditions" and thought none the worse of them if they were freshly invented. Just as the new May Day ritual was a pseudo-folk custom, so were the local festivals that became popular by the 1890s, particularly in western North America. Motivated by a desire both to meld a community out of a raggle-taggle assortment of newcomers and to attract additional settlers, civic fathers organized events such as the St. Paul Winter Carnival (which dates from 1885), the Pasadena Tournament of Roses (1889), the Portland Rose Festival (1909) and the Vancouver Exhibition (later the Pacific National Exhibition, 1910). Leaning on the time-honored artistic practice of using women to represent the "spirit" of a locality, the festivities typically involved the crowning of a queen. Although the queen was usually a member of the social elite (valued for her position rather than her beauty), there was always the possibility of an upset. In Sacramento in 1900, for example, a shopgirl named Miss McAdam was chosen by popular vote over Mrs. H. G. Smith, "society leader." If every boy was a potential president, every girl could hope to become queen of the local fete.

All these issues of democracy and class, art and commerce, gender and sex would eventually come together in the beauty contests of the 1920s. For it was then, in the decade after the First World War, that a craze for queens would suddenly spread throughout the western world. From Constantinopole to Calgary, from Pittsburgh to Gay Paree, the beauty queen was about to become the poster girl for an era that was drunk on its own possibilities.

*Facing page: Where a regular guy might see nothing but whistle bait, an artist was presumed to discern an aesthetic conjunction of line, form and shade. Early pageant promoters often employed artists as judges, in an attempt to put a cultured veneer on the proceedings.*

# Voilà, You Are Famous

"You are going to live a fairy tale," the strange little man promised. "A true fairy tale."

Dressed with the elaborate elegance of a bygone age, Monsieur de Waleffe might have stepped off the pages of a fairy tale himself. He was the prince with the glass slipper, who could lift a girl out of the ashes and draw her into a dazzling life of happily-ever-afters. He was an improbable fairy godmother who, with little more than a wave of his hand, could produce a rainbow of shimmering ball gowns in the latest Paris fashions. As the promoter of the biggest beauty contest in France, Monsieur de Waleffe held the key to instant success for one lucky young woman. And this year, 1928, he had chosen to open the magic portal for an aspiring actress named Raymonde Allain. "Just think, mademoiselle," he crowed. "You were unknown, *voilà* you are famous!"

It was enough to turn the head of even the most down-to-earth and sceptical fifteen year old, and witty, sharp-tongued Raymonde Allain was exactly that. Writing about the experience a few years afterward, she confessed to an abiding and vehement belief that "nothing could be sillier than a beauty contest." And yet that fateful afternoon had found her crowded into

---

**I wanted to have an extraordinary destiny, something very special in life.**

—Laurel Schaefer, Miss America 1972, reflecting on why she had chosen to enter beauty contests

---

*By the end of the nineteenth century, working women in Paris were organizing beauty contests among themselves. The queen of Les Halles market for 1899, seen in this illustration from* Illustré Soleil du Dimanche, *worked as a butcher. The contests were quickly taken over by civic authorities, and the women lost control of their events.* J.-L. Charmet

*Facing page: As the winner of a beauty contest at Atlantic City in 1921, sixteen-year-old Margaret Gorman found herself wrapped in Old Glory and wearing Liberty's crown.* UPI/Corbis-Bettmann

a back room at the *Journal de Paris* (where Monsieur de Waleffe, in everyday life, reigned as editor) along with dozens of made-up, teased-out, fussed-over young women and their anxious *mamans*. Why were they here, any of them? Why had some of them thought it worthwhile to make the long journey in from the provinces, just for a turn in front of the judges? In Raymonde's sardonic assessment, it certainly wasn't because they were much to look at. Some had obviously been pushed by their mothers

("victims of maternal blindness"), others by their friends and suitors, still others by the faint hope of being seen and "discovered" by producers.

As for Raymonde herself, she would confess only to having been pushed "by the devil." In this case, *le malin* had taken the dual form of her dance instructor and an artist who employed her as a model, both of whom had encouraged her to enter. But she was also propelled forward by her own waywardness. Her parents didn't approve of beauty contests, but who said they had to know? She was several months too young to enter and worked in the theater (the one occupation that was explicitly banned), but did she really have to advertise these misdemeanors? Watch me, chase me, catch me if you can. Breaking the rules just adds to the fun when you're young and in love with your own ambition.

And now her small act of daring had paid off with this disconcerting triumph. She had been named Miss France, a distinction that automatically earned her a berth in the Third International Pageant of Pulchritude and Ninth Annual Bathing Girl Review in far-off Galveston, a beach resort on the south coast of Texas. Once there, might she again defy the odds and find herself acclaimed as Beauty Queen of the Universe? For the moment, all she could think of was the steamship that would take her to America and the swish of the curtains as they revealed her, alone at center stage, to the admiring gaze of the entire world.

When Raymonde crept into the house that night and confessed what she had done, this seductive vision cast its spell over her parents. And so it was, scarcely two weeks

*Doing her best to uphold the honor of French fashions, Raymonde Allain (far left) appears in the winner's lineup wearing a stylish hat. Miss Canada (far right), the sixth-place finisher, was Irene Hill of Calgary. The winner—proclaimed Beauty Queen of the Universe—was Ella Van Hueson of Chicago.* Rosenberg Library, Galveston, Texas

*Facing page: For a girl who yearned to be the center of attention, it was hard to beat the Pageant of Pulchritude at Galveston. All along the seawall, crowds would stand for hours in the blazing sun to catch a glimpse of their favorites.* Rosenberg Library, Galveston, Texas

*Overleaf: "Frolic and fantasy" appears to have been the theme of Galveston's beachwear competition in 1923.* Photography Collection, Harry Ransom Humanities Research Center, The University of Texas at Austin

FOURTH ANNUAL BATHIN
GALVESTON ~ 1

IRL REVUE

JUNE 13-17, 1931

**12TH ANNUAL INTERNATIONAL BEAUTY PAGEANT**
GALVESTON   TEXAS

1920  1922  1924  1926  1928    *"The Glory of Beautiful Girlhood"*    1929  1927  1925  1923  1921

*Just as man had risen from the apes, so modern woman could be shown to have progressed through a decade of gradual undress.* Rosenberg Library, Galveston, Texas

afterward, that she found herself steaming across the Atlantic in the company of her mother and six other beauty queens from western Europe: Misses England, Belgium, Italy, Germany, Spain, even a Miss Luxembourg. Laden with this exotic cargo, the ship touched land in New Orleans and then dipped south to Vera Cruz, where amid threats of abduction by night and cascades of flowers by day, they picked up the local candidate, Miss Mexico. Another port of call, and Miss Cuba was added to the party. Then it was on to the United States of America, to be met by representative girls from all the major cities and states of the union. There, gathered under the hot sun of the Gulf Coast, stood the rhinestone royalty of two continents—*reines de beauté* "in industrial quantities."

From the beginning, Raymonde had had her doubts about the fairy-tale world into which, willy-nilly, she had been inducted. Why did everyone suddenly think they had the right to boss her around? "Have I become the queen of beauty in order to obey everybody?" she fretted. The journalists who interviewed her for the papers altered her biography and opinions to suit their own purposes; the press photographers who took her picture felt free to tamper with her appearance. ("Don't worry, mademoiselle," they said, as they fiddled with her hair. "Don't worry, we are artists.") Monsieur de Waleffe and the team of couturiers, shoe merchants and hairdressers that he assembled were even more purposeful in their interference. "How can anyone expect her to represent France if she doesn't follow *la mode française* to the last detail?" the hairstylist scolded, as she reached for her shears. Raymonde's luxurious locks, in which she took such pride, would have to be sacrificed to the gods of style.

"I didn't dare to resist," she lamented. "I didn't

> As an advertising campaign, the Pageant was, and is, a masterpiece, and it couldn't be bought for half-a-million dollars.
>
> —railroad spokesperson, expounding on the benefits of beauty contests, early 1920s

MISS AUSTRALIA 1927
Art Souvenir

Miss Australia 1927

Miss Phyllis von Alwy

F. VAUDRY-ROBINSON.

belong to myself. I now belonged to Parisian commerce." If Monsieur de Waleffe, in his absurd clothes, appeared to represent the oldest traditions of chivalry, Raymonde could see that he actually embodied the crassest, "most American" methods of contemporary business. He was, she concluded, nothing but a huckster, and he and his business partners intended to use her "like a lighted sign" to promote their own commercial *cum* patriotic interests. Even her virtue had taken on national significance. "People talked to me endlessly about my virginal air," she recalled with chagrin. " 'Your features reveal virginal beauty.' And 'your virginal grace.' And 'your virginal smile.' My virginity had become part of the patrimony of the fatherland."

In Texas, there were other interests to be served. The good reputation of the pageant itself had to be safeguarded against any suggestion of "worldly" behavior among the contestants. The girls were not to go out without their chaperons nor to speak to young people in the town. As for smoking a cigarette, that "didn't go over much better in Galveston than eating an apple had in Paradise," Raymonde wryly noted. But the greatest annoyance came with the discovery that the contest had been fixed in advance. Although Miss France was the clear favorite of the crowds who lined the beach to watch the "bathing girls" parade and packed the grand hall to see them model their gowns, the crown would go to big-boned Miss Chicago. Not only was she reputedly rich enough to return her two-thousand-dollar prize to the contest

*F. Vaudry-Robinson's* Art Souvenir *contained views of Miss Australia feeding a kangaroo, gracing the map of Tasmania and flying on a giant bird. By the 1950s, her successors had been given the serious tasks of encouraging immigration by the "better type" of settler and promoting the United Nations Children Appeal. Today, somewhat improbably, the Miss Australia program is run as a fund-raiser for the Spastics Society (a charity for the disabled) and is under pressure to admit men as full participants.* Australian Archives

*Overleaf: Beauty-contest promoters have always maintained that girls are judged in swimwear as a sign of their active good health. But poor Miss Toronto and her court look downright sickly compared to a flotilla of marathon swimmers (greased against the cold) who have just climbed out of Lake Ontario. Both photos date from around 1926.* City of Toronto Archives SC 233-1028M and SC 233-1028D

We like to see the daughters of the working class

*maintaining their beauty and physical fitness.*

—from a critique of beauty contests, *The Woman Worker*, Toronto, 1926

*Atlantic City is the apotheosis of publicity. It is the crescendo of horn-tooting.*

—from a report in the *New York Times,* 1929

organizers, she was also American and, as such, could be used to promote the economic interests of both the pageant and her homeland. Raymonde—now officially ranked as the second most beautiful female in the cosmos—would have to settle for the consolation of a thousand American dollars.

Would she have done it again? Not if her life had depended on it. But this kind of critical distance could only be gained through experience. For many other young women, the romance of the beauty queen still glittered as brightly as it once had for Raymonde herself. Fame, travel, glamour, cash—who wouldn't say yes to that! So what if it was all a little tacky and extravagant? The industrial age was like that—fast, glitzy, superficial, commercial. Live a little; catch the new beat. Welcome to the jazzin', jivin', tango-till-dawn spirit of the twenties.

By the end of the decade, beauty contests had been held in more than two dozen countries. In Australia (where the first beauty queen was crowned in 1908), a national contest was established in 1926. That same year, Montreal sent five prize winners to New York for a tour of Fox Studios and a fleeting, flickering screen debut in a newsreel. In Toronto, a civic contest at the Sunnyside Bathing Pavilion—"the poor man's Riviera"—drew a turnout of 475 young women in lamentably unflattering bathing costumes. The winner, statuesque Jean Ford of 5 Shannon Street, was garlanded like a monument and given a cup to take home.

By 1930, the fever had spread to South and Central America—Chile, Peru, Guatemala, Brazil. A Miss Universe competition in Sao Paulo that year boasted entries from Europe and the United States, though the crown went, inevitably, to the hometown gal. (The interests behind these things were always "nearly honest," as Raymonde Allain put it.) But no matter where the idea traveled around the world, the concept always seemed essentially American. It was as if beauty contests had all been stamped "Made in the U.S.A." Here, on display for all to see, were the quintessentially American values of competition and advancement through merit; here, under a gloss of feminine charm, was the good old American yen for turning a profit.

In a decade that was only too willing to be seduced by outrageous money-making stunts (such as pole sitting and dance marathons), beauty contests proved to be the ultimate publicity gimmick. Nothing, but nothing, opened wallets like a lineup of "bathing girls," and nowhere was this simple fact exploited with greater effect than in the flashy little resort town of Atlantic City, New Jersey. With the help of a hurricane that flattened the Gulf Coast, the Fall Frolique on the Boardwalk would eventually eclipse even Galveston's Pageant of Pulchritude to become the premiere event of its kind in the United States. First staged in 1921 in an attempt to draw people back to the beach after the Labor Day long weekend in September, the festivities included parades, concerts, sporting events, a fancy-dress ball and beauty contests galore, with prizes for kids, for men, for "professional" women (the stars of stage and screen) and, much to the delight of the crowds, for the prettiest of the eight beauty queens who had come to represent their respective communities. Sixteen-year-old Margaret Gorman of Washington, D.C. (30–25–32), with her Mary Pickford curls and open-hearted smile, was the choice of the panel of artists who served as judges. They wrapped her up in the Stars and Stripes and paraded her around the place as Miss America.

In 1922, when Margaret came back to defend her crown (unsuccessfully, as it turned out), the lineup of civic beauties had expanded from eight to fifty-eight, and a reporter at the scene found himself gasping at the "carnival of beauty" that "rippled, splashed, and sparkled until the thousands banked solidly on either flank [of the Boardwalk] were wild with enthusiasm." As for the contestants themselves, they were "jazz babies who shook the meanest kind of shoulders, pink-skinned beauties of all types who had come across the continent." But another onlooker—the venerable Samuel Gompers, longtime president of the American Federation of Labor—was stirred by more somber thoughts. Identifying Margaret Gorman as the most worthy candidate, he declared, "She represents the type of womanhood America needs—strong, red-blooded, able to shoulder the responsibilities of homemaking and motherhood. It is in her type that the hope of the country rests."

In the very best of fairy tales, they don't say things like that.

*The early Miss America contests were just one aspect of what a reporter described as a "carnival of beauty" that "ran riot on the resort's famous Boardwalk." In 1924, for example, the contestants were conveyed on elaborate floats (some said to be worth as much as $250,000) that rolled along to the pulsing beat of the fifty parade bands. In the days before motorized flatbeds, the floats were pulled by "slaves," the only African Americans to appear in the festival.* Princeton Antiques, Atlantic City

# Sex and the Single Flapper

Under normal circumstances, the jazz baby and the red-blooded mother of the nation might never even have met, much less found themselves embodied by one and the same young woman. But the twenties were no ordinary decade. Born in the euphoric optimism at the end of the First World War, the ebullient spirit of the age would eventually be subdued by the stock-market crash of 1929. Between these landmark events, society experienced the final stages of a transformation (begun before the war) that would result in a complete "restructuring" of the western world.

Over the span of two or three generations, an economy based on manual labor and small-scale production had been recast as an efficiency-oriented machine scaled for massive outputs. Industrialization drew workers from the farms and workshops to the factories and offices of burgeoning urban centers. Here, in the round-the-clock glare of city lights, life kept time with the throbbing beat of the internal combustion engine. When Henry Ford switched on the first "line production system" in 1910, he accelerated a chain of social consequences that would eventually revolutionize not only work and leisure but also almost every other aspect of human existence.

Change makes people anxious, and in the early decades of the century, a general atmosphere of anxiety found an outlet in a tut-tutting debate about the nature of women. In the old, established scheme of things, "true womanhood" had been a

*Despite the Victorian dictum that women belonged in the home, supporters of the women's suffrage movement had made a spectacle of themselves to gain attention for their cause. One of their tactics had been wearing sashes that advertised their views, similar to those seen here on the members of the Anti-Flirt Club. Organized in 1923 by Alice Reighly of Washington, D.C. (the woman in the print dress), the club enrolled girls who objected to being "embarrassed," or harassed, by men in automobiles and on street corners.*

*Although beauty-contest promoters could not have cared less about advancing the feminist cause, they nonetheless outfitted their contestants with suffrage-style sashes. For the girl who yearned to be wealthy or sexually free, liberation might seem to lie in becoming a beauty queen.* Library of Congress LC-USZ62-42082

well-defined ideal and a key to understanding Victorian society. Building on the notion that the sexes were not merely different from one another but actually opposite, nineteenth-century experts had described completely separate spheres for men and women. A real woman, they agreed, was naturally domestic, pious and refined. Her realm was within the home, where she lived her days in modest retirement, selfless service and patient submission to her lord and master. As one pundit put it, "The distinction of sex [puts men and women] in different classes of being. One is the force principle, the other is the beauty principle." Men were preordained to go out into the world and employ their genius in the service of power and wealth; women were to sit quietly by the fire and apply their feminine wiles to making life pleasant.

Alfred, Lord Tennyson, poet laureate of the nineteenth century, once summarized these oppositions in five portentous lines:

> *Man for the field and woman for the hearth;*
> *Man for the sword, and for the needle she;*
> *Man with the head, and woman with the heart;*
> *Man to command, and woman to obey;*
> *All else confusion.*

In point of fact, sitting quietly by the hearth was an impossible dream for many hard-working women. But mere reality could not dull the lustre of the middle-class ideal, which provided a common-sense vision of women's role that was widely shared. Even the suffragists (the feminists of the early twentieth century) generally agreed that the sexes were essentially and irrevocably distinct from each other.

For the most part, the doctrine of "separate spheres" was used to keep women in their place as social and political inferiors. But the suffragists gave the argument an unexpected twist. Women, they said, were not just different from men; they were morally superior. As natural-born caregivers, they were motivated by a mother's pure and instinctive love. As the "angels of the house," they were spared the

In 1885, no nice woman [had] any anatomy between her neck and her ankles.

—gynecologist Robert Latou Dickinson, 1932

base urges that, all too often, corrupted the dealings of men. For the truth was (as some suffrage leaders whispered) that the human male was naturally lascivious—constantly at the beck and call of his penis. A true Victorian woman, by contrast, was passionless, her body untroubled by unclean impulses.

It was by working from these precepts (among others) that the suffragists developed their political agenda. The vote should be extended to women, they argued, because female voters, as the moral betters of men, would clean up public life. They would take aim at the social and sexual evils that were threatening civilization—evils such as alcohol abuse ("intemperance"), prostitution ("white slavery") and sexually transmitted disease ("race suicide"). All these plagues were spread by the lust of men, at the expense of innocent women.

To me the Jazz Age signifies an age of freedom in thought and action. The average young person of today is not bound by the strict conventions which governed the actions of previous generations.

—young woman, University of Denver, 1926

Although the suffragists made only fitful progress toward addressing their social platform, they did attain their primary goal of votes for women. In many jurisdictions throughout the Western world, women were granted suffrage during or soon after the First World War. But no sooner was the goal in sight than the movement began to lose force. A new generation of women was coming of age, one that, with the natural ingratitude of youth, took the struggles of its foremothers for granted. Buoyed by the end of the War to End All Wars, invigorated by the recognition of women's contribution to the war effort and empowered by the vote, the rising generation literally danced to a different beat than the old folks. The racy new rhythms that blared out from the afternoon tango teas were frankly sensual.

And how the old guard clucked. "Anyone who says that 'youths of both sexes can mingle in close embrace'—with limbs intertwined and torsos in contact—without suffering harm

*Two young members of the National Women's Party make a show of doffing their hats as a token of their desire to be treated as equals by men, Washington, D.C., 1925.* Library of Congress LC F-81-36303

*Miss Yonk...*

lies," hissed a writer for the *Ladies' Home Journal* in the early twenties. "Add to this position the wriggling movement and sensuous stimulation of the abominable jazz orchestra with its voodoo-born minors and its direct appeal to the sensory center, and if you can believe that youth is the same after this experience as before, then God help your child." Indeed, divine intervention seemed the most likely defense against the many and varied excesses of the young—especially of young women.

Totally oblivious to the old fogeys' call for restraint, the jazz babies of the twenties were thirsting for experience. As one young woman put it in 1924, "women always used to take their look at life through a telescope—held stoutly in the hands of some male member of the family. Now they are permitted to get a closeup." And what they were privileged to experience was a whole new world of both work and pleasure. For the first time in history, a generation of urban girls was spilling out of the home to take up paid employment in factories, shops and offices. By the early years of the new century, nearly 60 percent of women aged sixteen to twenty in New York held jobs. In Toronto, where more than forty thousand single women had found employment by 1914, more than a third of that number maintained homes of their own. These trends accelerated into the twenties. Despite pitiful wages, poor possibilities for advancement and limited expectations (most still saw their lifework as marriage), these "bachelor girls" were exhilarated by their unprecedented freedom. "I was a lively girl, a devil," one of them admitted. "I was healthy, young and all that, and they used to say I was very pretty also."

*Facing page: A true daughter of her times, Miss Yonkers '24 confidently invites life to take her on its own terms. Her foremothers, by contrast, had viewed women's circumstance with greater suspicion.*
Library of Congress LC-USZ62 -37427

*In 1927, for the first time, Emily Post's 1927 etiquette manual included a chapter on "The Vanishing Chaperon." A decade later, she wistfully concluded that chaperonage had been "lost."*

*Two's Company — Three's a Crowd.*

FRED HESS & SON
ATLANTIC CITY, N.J.
124

Our New Radium $5.00
Home Permanent Wave
Bathing Beauty

COPYRIGHT
1924
H.W. CHERRY

In the old order of womanly refinement, a "lively girl" of marriageable age would have been tightly chaperoned. But the emancipated young working girl was out there on her own, rubbing shoulders with men of all kinds and conditions. She wasn't shy about it either, with her rouged lips, bared legs and uncorsetted body. In the euphemistic lingo of the decade, she had "It"; she had "oomph"— qualities that were not lost on male employers. As the proprietor of an employment agency explained, appearance was "100% important before all other qualifications" for girls who wanted work. What employers wanted were "the white skinned girls with thin and straight mouths. The prettier they are, the better their chances." An unmarried girl who was careful about her looks added to "the general attractiveness" of the office and made the customers want to return. An ill-dressed or married woman just couldn't turn the trick.

If pretty clothes were a necessity for the business girl, they also quickly became her all-consuming pleasure. For one naive young girl who came to the city to find work, the fashion parade at the office was pure intoxication. "Seeing girls wearing what looked to me like lovely evening dresses at work went to my head," she recalled. "I got the lowest-necked georgette blouse and the shortest skirt I could find and high heels and silk stocking[s] with roses on them and hennaed my hair and somehow I looked so different I began to act different. . . ." The original "sleepy time gal," she found herself staying out late and dropping all her "good old habits" in favor of new-found leisure-time amusements.

The pleasures of the evening hours all centered around men. (As one observer of working-girls' culture noted, "No amusement is complete in which *he* is not a factor.") And here again, appearance was the key to success. Pretty girls snared the best

*Bobbed haircuts, permanent waves and makeup were part of the brazen new style of the flapper generation. In the early part of the century, such "artifice" would have been out of the question for respectable women. Even in the twenties, many workplaces—and beauty contests—forbade the use of cosmetics. But by the end of the decade, the old prudishness had been dispelled, and the beauty industry took off.* Library of Congress LC-USZ62-79464

*Facing page: Dressing up in glamorous clothes (and the daydream of wealth this implied) was a staple pleasure of the working girl's life. Beauty-contest organizers catered to this taste by including evening-gown competitions on their programs. What did it matter if some of the gowns came straight off the rack? Add enough sequins, ribbons and lace, and they still might catch the eye of the judges— or a rich marriage prospect. Norma Smallwood (left), Miss America 1926, is said to have parlayed her stylish good looks into $100,000 in contracts and a proposal from an oilman.* Princeton Antiques, Atlantic City

*Keeping your balance twixt naughty and nice was a challenge that called for poise—a virtue that has always been highly valued by beauty-contest judges. Here, making a difficult task appear easy, are five real pros, full-time bathing beauties from the Sennett film studio in 1918.* Library of Congress LC-USZ62-63659

*Can anyone tell me what poise is? Does it have anything to do with submission?*

—protester at the Portland Rose Queen contest, 1994

husbands; pretty girls had more fun. Because women's wages were so low, girls couldn't afford expensive outings on their own. But by showing a little leg or batting their eyelashes in the right direction, they might catch the attention of promising young men with a little extra cash in their pockets. In return for a night of "treating," a girl might permit a good-night kiss or a little "petting," especially if her fellow showed some inclination toward marriage.

If a man pushed for more than a kiss and a squeeze, it was up to the girl to cool his ardor, and she was quite prepared to accept this responsibility. Writing from her vantage point as a twenties' coed, one young woman acknowledged the undoubted pleasures of smoking, dancing, "dressing décolleté" and petting. "The real enjoyment lies in the thrill we experience in these things," she admitted. But the situation did not become "alarming," as some adults feared, because the girl of the day never lost her poise. "She knows her game and can play it dexterously. She is armed with sexual knowledge [and] . . . secure in the most critical situations—*she knows the limits,* and because of her safety in such knowledge *she is able to run almost the complete gamut of experience.*" According to the updated double standard, a passionate maiden could express her desires as long as she kept her head.

The young women who espoused these modern views saw themselves—not the old-time suffragists—as the vanguard of women's liberation. As one of them put it, any girl "who has the vitality of young womanhood, who feels pugilistically inclined when called the 'weaker sex,' who resents being put on a pedestal and worshipped from afar, *who wants to get into things for herself,* is a flapper." She, and she alone, "is responsible for the advancement of woman's condition in the world." Now that the old inequities had been resolved through the granting of the vote, there was no further need for collective action by an organized movement. Now was the time for women to claim their place in the world through their own individual brilliance. In the inspired phrase of one commentator, the time was ripe for acts of "magnificent and flaming audacity"—acts that might include entering a beauty contest. If Amelia Earhart could fly a plane, if Gertrude Ederle could swim the English Channel, surely nothing could hold a woman back except her own lack of daring.

*Facing page: Like a debutante at a coming-out ball, a beauty contestant is presented to society in Atlantic City, sometime in the 1920s.* Princeton Antiques, Atlantic City

*You never get nothing by being an angel child,*
*You'd better change your ways an' get real wild.*
—blues singer Ida Cox, "Wild Women Don't Have the Blues"

# Sand, *Surf and Stardust*

In cold point of fact, it wasn't to be that easy. Throughout the teens and the twenties, the lives of most "business girls" offered remarkably little scope for gestures of self-liberation, flaming or otherwise. You could be as audacious as you liked and still lose your job when you married or reached age thirty-five. Ambition alone couldn't help you survive on a bare-bones minimum wage—set at $12.56 per week for a girl in Ontario in 1920 (well below the going rate for a male). And daring was certainly no guarantee of an easy rise to the top in a world where "man" was still virtually synonymous with "boss." Professions like accounting, law and medicine remained male strongholds, and women's access to advanced education was restricted by custom and, sometimes, by law. In the United States, for example, the number of female physicians actually declined between 1920 and 1929 because many hospitals refused to accept women for internships.

All this is clear with hindsight. But at the time, people were dazzled by the ebullient sunshine of postwar optimism, and any shadow of worry or doubt was easily overlooked. Surely this was a time to "pack up your troubles," as the song advised, and make the most of the opportunities that *were* open to you. Work wasn't the sum total of a girl's ambitions, after all. If she couldn't get ahead in business, she still had a chance to make something of herself during her leisure hours.

*Despite a swimming costume that could scarcely be called risqué, this nineteenth-century bathing beauty was hot stuff in her day. The caption reads, "Waiting for Willie to take her in the Pacific at Santa Monica, Cal."* H. F. Rile. Santa Monica Public Library Archives

*Facing page: If the gals wanted someone to look at them in their daring beach attire, the guys at a Washington beach were more than willing to oblige. (Thirty years later, in the fifties, the audience for an event like this would have been almost entirely female.)* Library of Congress LC-F8 19121

Greetings from *Long Beach*

BATHING IN THE SURF.

Until around the turn of the century, Long Beach, California, was a quiet seaside resort where holiday-makers came to sun themselves and splash around in the waves. But the new commercial culture affected leisure like everything else, and the beach was quickly transformed into a metropolis of mechanized merriment. In California, as elsewhere, beauty pageants were a surefire draw with the crowds, attracting both spectators and participants by the hundreds. Archives of the Historical Society of Long Beach

*"Miss Swim" in name only, this turn-of-the-century pinup would have been sunk in the sea, impeded not only by her full-length suit but also by tight corsetting.* Library of Congress LC-USZ-35383

The whole notion that working-class women were entitled to leisure was, in itself, exciting and new. In the old economy of home-based production, there had been no formal limitations on a woman's hours of labor. "A man may toil from sun to sun, but a woman's work is never done" was a time-honored truth. But in the new economy of wage labor, working women were legally entitled to time away from their jobs—hours and even days that they could shape to their hearts' desire. As one young bookbinder recalled, life had been a gray routine of "sleep and eat and hurry off to work," until the eight-hour workday brought her first hint that there was, as she put it, "such a thing as pleasure." Through careful economy, she could sometimes afford to kick up her heels at a Saturday-night dance or squander a whole afternoon at the seashore.

If a gal wanted to find an outlet for her pent-up ambitions, there was no better place for her than the local beach resort or amusement park. At Atlantic City, Coney Island and dozens of other places around the continent, an orgy of entertainments was on offer at prices to fit the most modest of budgets. From the "freaks" to the Ferris wheels, everything was designed to defy the restrictions and repressions of the daily grind. Liberated by the salt breezes and the carnival atmosphere, a factory girl could elevate herself to the status of a stenographer, and a strait-laced schoolmarm might find herself wading into the ocean, still fully clothed.

"Honey, you make me do what you know I oughtn't to/Oh, when it's moonlight, down on the Boardwalk." So ran the lyrics of one musical tribute to the Atlantic City resort. The seaside was risqué, the kind of place where a nice girl could sip highballs with a man she had met that very afternoon. She might even marry him, if he were smarter or classier or richer than the boys she knew back home. Mix and mingle; strut your stuff. You never knew who might be in the audience. And even if no promising young men were overwhelmed by your charms, you could still experience the thrill of making a fashion statement.

Fashion was the flapper's politics. For decades, the old-time feminists had struggled against the oppressions of nineteenth-century styles. At a time when whalebone corsets made a labor of every breath and heavy, ankle-length skirts frustrated a purposeful step, the reformers had campaigned for lighter, healthier modes of dress. But society was aghast at the thought of unrestrained female flesh, and their crusade for "rational dress" had met with little success. Now a generation of silly young things had transformed the style overnight by freeing their limbs and lungs with unrepentant delight.

Improper! Indecent! the clergy wheezed, but the daring flappers would hear nothing of it. "Why should the fact that a girl [shows her] legs arouse the wrong kind of impulses in a man?" one young woman asked. "Does he think we travel on wheels?" No one had a right to tell her—a self-respecting business girl who earned her own living—how she ought to dress. And the same thing held for the revealing new styles in swimwear. Gone were the bulky costumes of the past with their long skirts and leggings of heavy silk or wool. Today's active woman demanded a simple, form-fitting outfit in a lightweight knit that literally got her into the swim. In the interests of modesty, she completed her look with sheer stockings that completely encased her lower limbs.

Even so, the new costume was too much for the defenders of public rectitude. When competitive swimmer Annette Kellerman introduced the style to the public in 1907, she was immediately arrested. Well into the twenties, a woman could be sent to jail for baring her legs on the beach or even for rolling her stockings too far below her knees. In Atlantic City, the city fathers went to the trouble of defining the maximum allowable gap twixt suit and hose, and then hired "beach censors" to patrol the strand, armed with police batons and measuring tapes.

One of the maidens to fall afoul of this law was a holidaymaker from Los Angeles named Louise Rosine. Ordered, not unkindly, to cover up her legs, Miss Rosine declared that she most certainly would *not*. Then, in a scene straight out of the Keystone Cops, she punched the poor beach censor right in the chops. "The city has no right to tell me how I shall wear my stockings," she proclaimed in her own defense. "It is none of their darn business. I will go to jail first." And so she did, all the while issuing outraged

*Overleaf: In the nineteenth century, people did not visit the seaside to swim. Instead, they came to "take the waters" (i.e., stand around half-submerged), an activity that was thought to be healthful. Those with a special aversion to exercise—or to being observed—could have themselves drawn into the sea in a wheeled cabin called a "bathing machine." But sooner or later you had to emerge and expose yourself to the world.*

*When beachwear was modernized in the teens and twenties, exposure continued to be an issue. Like many other seaside towns, Washington employed a beach cop to discipline men who bared their chests and women who showed too much leg.* Library of Congress LC-USZ62-60644, LC-USZ62-99824

Policeman, policeman, do your duty,

Here comes Mabel, the bathing beauty.

She can do the rhumba,

She can do the splits

She can pull her dress right up to her hips.

How many inches did she lift it?

—Skipping song

*In the recent past in America, the sex demands of women have been negligible, but that is no longer true. At no point has what we may justly call emancipation been more significant.*

—Sociologists Groves and Ogburn, in their study of American marriage, 1928

statements about her right to bare her knees. Surely, she and other women had a right to live comfortably and without shame in their beautiful, sexual, female bodies. If, as the pundits asserted, "modern women [had] awakened to the knowledge that they are sexual beings," why in Heaven's name shouldn't they be free to look sexy?

The case for women's freedom was made, insistently, by a generation of young women who crowded onto the beaches in their cling-fit suits and rolled-down hose. When no one wants to listen, actions speak louder than words, and running around in a one-piece swimsuit spoke volumes. It said that women could show themselves in public without being whores. It said that bodies were made for pleasure and play (within decent limits, of course). As a writer for *Vogue* suggested about 1915, the "bathing-girl . . . deserves the credit for firing the first shot in the Battle of Modern Dress." A few years later, the same publication gushed that "the modern girl" had emerged "triumphant" from this struggle and was henceforth empowered to wear whatever she liked to the seashore.

The bathing-beauty contest was a perfect opportunity to wave the standard of women's sartorial emancipation. An old-fashioned lady would have blanched at the thought of putting herself on display. But a saucy young flapper enjoyed the thrill of feeding the public gaze. Just standing up there was a cock of the snoot at all the old fogeys who thought that women should be kept under a shroud to protect society from moral rot. Entering a seaside beauty contest was a playful way to suggest that women's bodies should be out in the light, where they could be enjoyed and appreciated.

If the contestants were squeamish about being ogled by onlookers and scrutinized by male judges, they did not voice a protest. Perhaps no one bothered to ask them how they felt, or perhaps they were so used to being assessed by men that they didn't think to object. At work and at play, the life of a working girl was a round-the-clock beauty contest, in which men did the looking and women did their best to be worth looking at. A beauty pageant took this everyday transaction and turned it into a sport, with the added allure of glittering rewards that real life was unlikely to afford.

To a girl stuck in a dead-end job, with no way out but a lacklustre marriage, a beauty contest could look like the rhinestone road to the life of her dreams. In an instant, the winner would be plucked from obscurity and flung into the firmament of stars. Her name would make the headlines; her picture would fill the rotogravure

*Facing page: A judge assists Miss Maine off the scale at the Miss America weigh-in, sometime during the 1920s. At that time, formal judging criteria had not been established, and it was left up to the judges (nearly always male) to decide how the girls should be ranked. At Atlantic City in 1922, a panel of artists attempted to rate them on a numerical scale, based on the precise measurements of facial features and body parts. According to two-time Miss America judge Norman Rockwell, "The judge who thought it up had a wonderful time measuring all the girls," but his system did not work. "We found you can't judge a woman's beauty piecemeal; you have to take the whole woman at once." Who would have guessed?* Library of Congress LC-USZ62-70601

of the Sunday *Times*. Crowds would meet her at the station; rich men would vie for her hand. New York impresarios and Hollywood producers would attempt to outdo each other in their offers of fame and fortune. It had happened before; why couldn't it happen again?

Take Clara Bow, for example. The quintessential sex symbol of the decade, the waifish "It Girl" received more fan mail than any other Hollywood actress in the late twenties; yet her life had begun in a dismal Brooklyn tenement. Her father, a sometime waiter and handyman, was frequently unemployed; her mother was mentally unstable and prone to fits of violence. Of the three children born to the Bows, only Clara survived childhood. Miserably lonely and with little hope for the future, she left school in grade eight and picked up jobs wherever she could, working first at a hotdog stand on Coney Island and then, briefly, as receptionist for an abortionist. "I wasn't much of nothin' and didn't have nobody," she said, but there was always one place she could go to feel better. "That was the motion pictures."

Like many another young woman in straitened circumstances, Clara entered into the Tinseltown fantasy with her whole heart. In her mind's eye, she became one of Mack Sennett's lively bathing beauties or the kiss-curled and comely Mary Pickford. In 1921, this impossible dream seemed poised to come true when she won a beauty contest sponsored by a group of fan magazines. First prize was an acting job in the movies. Never mind that Clara's footage ended up on the cutting-room floor (not to be released until after she was a star); never mind that she pounded the pavement for months before landing a second part; never mind that she eventually made a name for herself through her own energy and talent. The contest went down in fanzine history as Clara's big break, the turning point in a fabulous rags-to-riches saga. Who might be next?

Entering a beauty contest could not be confused with having a plan for your life. That would have called for a strategy; this was more of a lark. But in an era that offered young women few outlets for their ambition, a faint hope of getting ahead was clearly better than none.

*Adrienne Dore, Miss Los Angeles for 1925, headed straight to Hollywood, where she was made over in the image of Clara Bow (left). But, unlike her idol, she didn't have "It" and was never heard from again.* Photofest/Icon

# Motion Picture

APRIL

1 Shilling

Love Scenes
That Have
Come
True

Wally Beery's
Lowdown
On
Happiness

Why
Beauty
Winners
Fail

MARLAND
STONE

# The Wicked Age

The young women who entered bathing-beauty contests in the twenties had sand between their toes and stardust in their hearts. They put themselves on display because they wanted to—because showing yourself off in a bathing suit had nothing to do with the dark days of the past and everything to do with the bright, new promised land of the future. Exactly what that future would hold, or what their role in it would (or should) be, they probably couldn't have said. Did they want children? Careers? Lovers? Husbands? Who knew what it might finally mean to be "emancipated"? But whatever it turned out to be, the aspiring, desiring girls on the beach were up for the challenge.

"Nothing is settled in the woman's mind," a commentator named Lorine Pruette noted in 1931. "She is having to work out new ways of living, about which there are still many disputes. She has not the ready-made justifications of the men."

In the social laboratory of a rapidly changing society, entering a beauty contest was a slap-happy, seat-of-the-pants experiment. (If I do this, will anything change? Is this the magnificent act that will remake my prospects?) At the same time, it was also a cheeky, cheerful way to butt into the learned disputes about women and their inner-most natures. In a public debate that was monopolized by gray-bearded experts, the voices of young women were seldom, if ever, heard. No one asked them to give Sunday

*A seasoned trouper at age fifteen, "Rosebud" (later Joan) Blondell already had a realistic assessment of her selling points. "I had a good, big chest," she said, "the kind garbagemen whistle at." So when her father's vaudeville troupe ran short of cash in 1926, she capitalized on her assets to win the Miss Dallas contest. First prize was two thousand dollars, enough to get the theater company back to New York.* Photofest/Icon

*Facing page: "America, one may truthfully say, has gone beauty-contest mad," this fanzine announced in 1927. Of the thousands of girls who were crowned each year "from Maine to Florida, from New York to San Francisco," most appeared to have their hearts set on the silver screen.*

*Facing page: Also-rans in the Long Beach Bathing Beauty Pageant for 1926, these young women give the photographer their best, on the off chance they will catch the eye of someone important.* Archives of the Historical Society of Long Beach

*Our objection to beauty contests is that they are used merely as a means of advertising. . . . We dislike the idea that the daughters of the working class shall be the victims of commercialized beauty affairs.*

—*The Woman Worker,* Toronto, 1926

sermons or explain their views to the press. But when they stood up on the podium in their swimwear, all the papers for miles around wanted to take their pictures. In a culture that was learning to frame its meanings through the camera lens, bathing beauties created a provocative image of womanhood that carried more weight than thousands of pages of text. When their bodies talked, the eyes of the world turned.

Exactly what the world saw was another question. For as the bright-and-beautiful Raymonde Allain had astutely pointed out, the beauty queen did not belong exclusively to herself. In particular, she did not control the creation and interpretation of her own likeness. As soon as the beauty queen took up her public role (what Raymonde ruefully called her *"existence de symbole"*), she became a blank screen on which anyone and everyone felt free to project his or her own message. "Through me," she complained, "men loved, hated, [and] contested a thousand things that had nothing to do with myself." Was this glory, she lamented, "to be taken for what one is not?" The worst offenders, in her view, were the men who ran beauty contests and who saw the girls merely as vehicles for advancing their own commercial interests. "They pretend to honor a young woman," Raymonde charged, "but in fact, they just expose her, merchandise her" like any other product.

What a young woman needed most, she said, was not the flattery and fuss of becoming a beauty queen. Instead, she should be "left alone to become herself," with appropriate guidance and help. She certainly didn't need a bunch of suits taking her in their grip and making "the conquest of her liberty" even harder to accomplish.

For the men who organized beauty contests, helping young women take charge of their lives was nowhere on the agenda. This was business, after all. The bottom line that counted most was not tucked into a swimsuit; it was in the accountant's month-end statement of profits and losses. If the girls helped to sell the sponsors' products— be it newspapers, French fashions or seaside hotel suites—they were a success. If they didn't, they were nothing but a darned nuisance.

Running a beauty contest was tricky, and the girls couldn't be counted on to make it easier. What the occasion called for was a carefully brewed concoction of sunshine, soft sex, noble sentiments and razzmatazz that pricked the nose of propriety without actually giving offense. But it was difficult to keep the right spin on things if the girls got out of line, and Atlantic City in 1923 was a classic case in point. That year, the city played host to a field of seventy-four candidates, each and every one of whom said they would cheerfully bypass marriage for a chance at a career in the movies.

Among this bumptious company was Miss St. Louis, Charlotte Nash—"lovely and unspoiled daughter of the great American West"— who claimed to have her dimples insured for a cool hundred grand. No retiring maiden, Miss Nash produced advertising fans, distributed by Yellow Cab, on which she touted herself as the "Popular Favorite." As so she was, it seems, with a rich theater magnate, Fred G. Nixon-Nordlinger by name, whom she married within a year of her fourth-place finish. Her idyll ended in Paris in 1931, when her husband was shot dead, and the former Miss St. Louis was tried and acquitted as a murderess.

This was hardly the ideal American Girl, "artistic and refined," whom the local Chamber of Commerce had set out to find. Nor, when all the facts were in, was the first-ever Miss Alaska, who turned up in Atlantic City looking remarkably smart after a five-thousand-mile journey by every known means of transport, including dogsled. The Chamber was not amused to learn that she had actually motored down from New York, nor that she was the wife of a publicity-hungry "physical culture" expert. (Marriage was not yet against the rules of the Miss America contest, but it did raise awkward questions about a beauty maid's innocence.) When contest officials tried to shunt her aside, Miss Alaska sued, claiming to have suffered "humiliating discrimination" at the hands of the pageant.

But who had humiliated whom? In the eyes of the local hotelmen, the contestants were to blame for besmirching the reputation of their fair city. Pointing to an "epidemic" of women around the world who were seeking "personal aggrandizement and publicity by participating in various stunts," the hotelmen accused this disreputable element of ruining their high-minded pageant. "Many of the girls who come here turn out bad later," a spokesman for the hoteliers complained, and regardless of where their

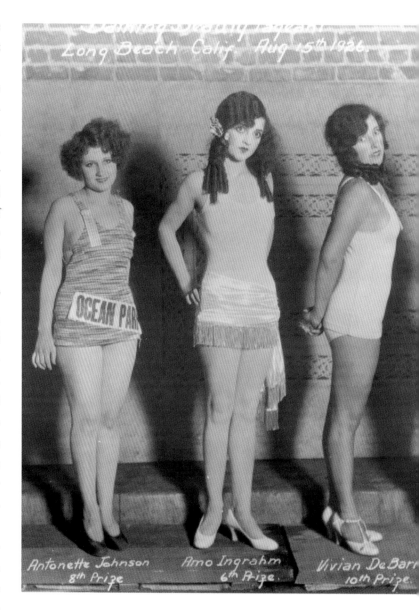

Long Beach Calif Aug 15th 1926

Antonette Johnson
8th Prize

Amo Ingrahm
6th Prize.

Vivian DeBarr
10th Prize.

China's Perfect Girl: Miss Yarlock Lowe, a Chinese student at the University of California, enjoys the distinction of being the only physically perfect girl among 500 female students. She underwent a careful examination and was declared to be perfect not only in health, but to be the most symmetrical of the entire class. The examining physicians were amazed at this, since, they say, a Chinese woman who even approached physical perfection has never before been recorded.

—*Leslie's Illustrated Weekly,* 1915

misdeeds might have occurred, they still reflected badly on Atlantic City.

The girls were running amok, and something would have to be done about it. But, meanwhile, the Atlantic City officials could thank their lucky stars that they hadn't suffered the embarrassment that befell Flushing, New York. Talk about attracting the wrong type of contestant! The fiasco began in the spring of 1924 when the "Green Twigs," a group of socially prominent ladies, set out to choose a queen for a community fiesta. The winner was to be elected by popular ballot. Early on, the tally showed a most disquieting trend—a girl named Dorothy Derrick was pulling ahead. In some ways, Miss Derrick was a model candidate: granddaughter of a Methodist bishop, an honor student and, as the New York *Times* reported, "handsome in her way." But Miss Derrick was also black.

After another day of voting, Miss Derrick had fallen to third, and the lead had been taken over by Violet Meyer, whose father was a street-corner newspaper vendor. Miss Meyer was a Jew. Completely flustered by this uncalled-for turn of events, the Green Twigs suspended the contest. (It was later reinstated by local merchants, with Miss Derrick in second place and Miss Meyer out of contention.)

The Twigs would never explain why they'd called off the voting. But did anything have to be said? Was it not a matter of plain common sense that neither a Negro nor a Jew could win a beauty contest? The finest and best of humans, in the view of modern science, were descended from the vigorous Nordic peoples of northern Europe. On this point, the experts concurred. As Havelock Ellis had explained in his authoritative study of sexual attraction, published in 1905, there was, in nature, an absolute, objective scale of beauty along which the races were ranked, with Negroes at the bottom and Europeans at the top. This explained, he said, why men of "the lower races" admired white women more than their own, and why dark-skinned women used powder to lighten their complexions. When it came right down to it, white was beautiful.

By allowing women of all the wrong types to rise to prominence, beauty contests posed a threat to the natural order of things and put middle-class women, like the Green Twigs, in a tizzy. Within days of the Flushing debacle, the reform-minded ladies of the Trenton YWCA, girded in righteousness, issued a ringing condemnation of all beauty pageants. Avoiding any reference to murky racial theories, their statement trod the moral high ground of womanly purity. The trouble with bathing-beauty parades—

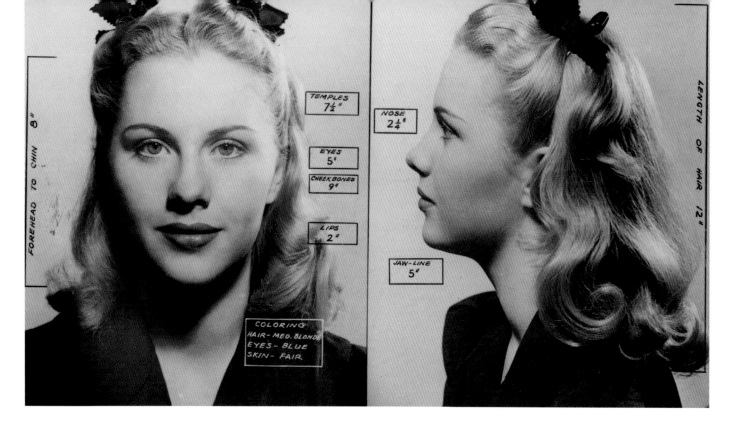

Inside image labels:
TEMPLES 7½"
NOSE 2¼"
EYES 5'
CHEEK BONES 9"
LIPS 2"
JAW-LINE 5"
FOREHEAD TO CHIN 8"
LENGTH OF HAIR 12"
COLORING
HAIR— MED. BLONDE
EYES— BLUE
SKIN— FAIR

and Atlantic City was the worst—was the threat these spectacles posed to "girl welfare." As the self-appointed guardians of the working girl's interests, the Y (and other groups of the same ilk) undertook to protect young women from worldly dangers.

Whether they knew it or not, girls who entered beauty contests faced grave moral threats. Young women should use their bodies to serve the public good; they must stand as shining exemplars of Motherhood. By forgetting their sacred calling of modesty and restraint, girls removed the holy mantle of "pure womanhood." What was revealed by their reckless disrobing was the body of a tart, fit for little else but "a career that led to moral and mental destruction." Although girls might think of beauty contests as an exciting amusement, they were actually a "destroying factor," in league with white slavers and the dark forces of race suicide.

In the weeks and months that followed this outburst, clouds of brimstone swirled over Atlantic City and other seaside resorts, as women's organizations and church groups decried the moral dangers posed by beauty contests. "The saddest feature of the affair," said Dr. Lake of the Ocean City Camp Meeting Association, "is the willingness of a few businessmen to profiteer on the virtues of those of tender years." But in Atlantic City, the businessmen's sorrow was that all the bad press would ruin their

*In 1940, Max Factor, Jr., "Hollywood's beauty authority," developed this prototype of the "All-American Face." In his view, blonde, fair-skinned Mary Parker perfectly represented "the beauty norm" for all American girls, in regards to complexion, facial structure and measurements. Anyone who deviated from this norm (through ethnicity or race) was naturally consigned to second place.*
Photofest/Icon

*Overleaf: Miss Indian America takes a dignified view of the proceedings as King Neptune (Eddie Dowling) crowns Miss America 1927 (Lois Delander). Always kept in the background, Miss Indian America was expected to provide a ceremonial presence but was not invited to enter the contest.* Princeton Antiques, Atlantic City

Probably even patriotism does not demand of us an admiration for the beauty of the very first American girls——the dusky darlings of our primitive tribes. These earliest American girls were not endowed with the fatal gift of beauty as we understand it.

—Alexander Black, *Miss America*, 1898

*Facing page: Mae West's play* The Wicked Age, *or* The Contest *bombed in New York in 1927. A few years later, when this photograph was taken, she was one of Hollywood's leading lights. Never had the American dream shone with more splendor.*

Photofest/Icon

profits and leave them accountable for the pageant's deficit. The mood grew even sourer in 1925, when a New York newspaper, the *Graphic,* published claims that the Miss America contest was corrupt. By the time the accusations were apologetically withdrawn, three years afterward, the Atlantic City contest had been dropped, rejected by its sponsors as a "worn out and useless" idea, and a similar event at Rockaway amusement park had also been canceled. The Galveston pageant was gone by 1931.

But if the firestorm of protest put the promoters off, at least one person was drawn to the smoke of scandal. Her name was Mae West and, in the fall of 1927, she was resuming her theatrical career after a brief and unscheduled break—ten days in jail for staging an "obscene," and extremely profitable, play entitled *Sex.* Her new offering, which she wrote, produced and directed, was called *The Wicked Age,* and it featured a rumbustious flapper named Babe (played by Miss West, of course) who attains fabulous fame and fortune by winning a beauty contest. Too old at thirty-four to be part of the "queen scene" herself, Mae nonetheless had a sure grasp of its dynamics. All the real-life actors were put up on the boards—the town boosters ("All is fair in love, war and real estate"), the reformers ("The fall of every great nation . . . has been preceded by the immodesty of its womanhood"), and the rising generation of girls who rejected the faux sexlessness of their elders ("You can't smoke a cigarette," Babe shouted at her mother—"you can't rouge your lips—you can't take a drink— you can't breathe but you're [still] wicked").

Like her creator, Babe the beauty queen was determinedly, exuberantly wicked. "I want to be bad," she rages at her prissy father. "I'm sick and tired of trying to live the life you want me to live. . . . I want to be filthy low—vile—call it anything you please—but God I want to live my own life." Most of all, she wants to experience and enjoy the rewards of her own sexual power. She wants work; she wants money; she wants her choice of rich men. With West as her fairy godmother, her wishes are granted. But "the wicked age" still threatens her with its evil spell. In an age when "the exploitation of the female form" is the surest route to commercial success, does it count as a victory if you end up exploiting yourself?

I wrote the story myself. It's all about a girl who lost her reputation but never missed it.

—Mae West

# Daydream
## *Believers*

*In* the early months of 1929, the twenties were still in full roar, and the serious business of selling fun was booming as never before. Even without its beauty contest, Atlantic City had not lost its knack for drawing in the masses, siphoning off their spare cash, and sending them home sunburned and relaxed. The living was easy at the seashore. In the bedazzled eyes of one journalist, Atlantic City stood as both product and proof of the new industrial economy; the resort was, he said, "an iridescent bubble on the surface of our fabulous prosperity."

By year's end, the bubble had burst, and the optimism of the Jazz Age had fizzled like a dud firecracker. When the stock market crashed on September 3, the economy jolted to a halt, not just at the seaside but everywhere. Throughout the western world, factories closed, steel plants laid off workers, shipyards were silent. In the cities, people went hungry because they could not afford to buy food; on the farms, people lost their land because they could not sell enough to pay their bills. By 1934, the national income of the United States was little more than half what it had been five years earlier. By 1935, the crisis had deepened, and so things went on, year by year, until the outbreak of the Second World War.

The party was over, and the twenties' favorite party girl, the flapper, no longer gave expression to the public mood. In her place now stood a more womanly woman,

*Through the bleak years of the Dirty Thirties, beauty contests invited viewers to escape into a fantasy of wealth. Here, Marilyn Meseke, Miss America for 1938, poses outside the Dream Home on Million Dollar Pier in Atlantic City.* Princeton Antiques, Atlantic City

*Facing page: In 1930, the curve was queen, as evidenced by Galveston's lineup of international beauties.* Library of Congress LC-USZ62-348

MISS CANADA'S GREATEST GIFT
TO THE MOTHER-COUNTRY
HEALTH IN THE FORM OF FRUIT

*Miss Canada—the apple of everyone's eye—held center stage in this display, which was designed to promote the sale of Canadian fruit to England around 1930.* London News Agency Photo Ltd., National Archives of Canada

*Facing page: When a producer put out a call for "Miss Perfection of 1938" to headline an upcoming film, he was flooded with applicants, including at least one beauty-contest winner. Louise Small (second from the left in the saucy two-piece outfit) claimed the honors as Miss America for 1934, a year when at least three "national" titles were awarded in the U.S.* Photofest/Icon

with a bosom and hips, her curves augmented by the latest advances in foundation garments. As one observer noted at the time, "so striking was the change between the ideal figure of 1929 and that of 1933 that one might almost have thought a new anatomical species had come into being." But while women reshaped their bodies to fit the new mode, they did not completely abandon their flapper spirit. Tempered though it now was by hard times, the audacity of the twenties' generation still found expression in women's adult lives.

We can see it, for instance, in the fact that union membership among women in the United States increased more than three-fold during the thirties, from 250,000 to 800,000, or almost 20 percent of the female workforce. It took guts to sign up and face the boss's wrath or walk the picket line, if it came to that. For some women, whether unionized or not, just showing up for work each day was an act of rebellion. Married women were not supposed to work outside the home, especially at a time when so many men were without jobs. By depriving a breadwinner (i.e., a man) of an income, a working wife stood condemned of taking food from his kids—and for no very good reason, since her earnings were presumed to be spent on frills. But despite this insistent pressure, a significant minority of women went right on with their jobs to provide such frills as milk and shoes for their own children.

It would be foolish to pretend that the Depression was good for women. Poverty is not kind to anyone, and the majority of working women were poorer than ever. Wages, already inhumanely low, fell lower, and women's average annual earnings were still only half of men's. Hours of work remained long for both sexes—fifty to fifty-four hours per

The Cinderella legend is America's favorite fairy tale and the [film] industry's attempts to blast its power are rather half-hearted.

—Margaret Thorp, *America at the Movies,* 1939

week were not uncommon. Women's opportunities for advancement, already limited, were curtailed even further as hard times reinforced the prejudice against women in high-paying, high-status jobs.

If the young women of the twenties had been "all dressed up with nowhere to go," their counterparts ten years later didn't even have the benefit of dress-up clothes. All roads led to Nowhere, and some girls (a few hundred thousand of them) figured that it didn't really matter which way they headed. Like much larger numbers of dispossessed young men, they rode the rails and survived by any means at hand, always on the move, occasionally on the lam. According to one female hobo, the stories of these women were all very much alike—"no work, a whole family on relief, no prospects of marriage, the need for a lark, the need for freedom of sex and of living, and the great urge to know what other women were doing." "Sure that their sex would win them a way about," they indulged their "tough-girl" tastes for autonomy, self-expression and good times.

But for their stay-at-home sisters (by far the majority), these youthful desires were fulfilled only in dreams, and Hollywood stood poised, as ever, to feed their fantasies. "I'll bet every girl wishes she was the Greta Garbo type," said one star-sozzled fan. For others it was Joan Crawford ("I watch every little detail of how she's dressed, and her make-up, and also her hair") or Marlene Dietrich or Bette Davis or Katharine Hepburn. Blonde bombshells like Jean Harlow and Mae West (who made her

*Miss Shearer likes breakfast in bed, thin sandwiches spread with jam,*
*lying in a tub of warm water, raw vegetable salads,*
*and yellow roses.*

—*Look*, 1937

movie breakthrough in 1933) set a vogue for platinum hair and, against the trend of the times, kept storekeepers busy dispensing peroxide.

Women's movies were big box office during the thirties. Out of a total weekly audience in the United States of 85 million (or two-thirds of the population), a majority of the ticket buyers were female. This meant, as one producer put it, that women "set the type of picture that will go." And what went was not just glamour and luxe, though audiences certainly demanded the pleasures of opulence. Women also wanted their heroines to live with panache. Let Dietrich swagger in top hat and tails; let Garbo live with two men. Let Rosalind Russell dump Cary Grant and then choose to marry him again. The heroines of thirties' movies made up their minds for themselves, and even if they were married off in the end (as convention demanded), it didn't necessarily mean they'd been tamed. In her movie debut as a Gay Nineties' saloon keeper, Mae West was asked by her new screen husband if he could hold her hand. "It ain't heavy," the bride drawled in reply. "I can hold it myself."

On screen and off, Hollywood's new female stars were sexy, sassy and assertive, and the public loved them for it. They were also just plain rich. In 1935, a year when the average working woman earned $525, Mae West's audacity netted her $480,833. To the girls in the ten-cent seats in the movie house, the impossible dream of stardom glittered more brightly than ever. And perhaps it wasn't impossible, for the fan magazines (now with weekly sales in the millions) were brimming with the Cinderella stories of Hollywood's leading ladies. Joan Crawford had begun as a shop girl; Olivia de Havilland was "discovered" in a high school play; the young Barbara Stanwyck had toiled in the back row of the chorus. If you were a little nobody with no prospects (and what girl wasn't in the Dirty Thirties?), you might already have taken your first step on the highway to greatness.

If Hollywood is in the business of manufacturing dreams, the fantasy of instant stardom was its most alluring and saleable product during the thirties. By mid-decade, as Margaret Thorp reported in her sharp-tongued study *America at the Movies,* southern California was overrun with "seekers for glamour," many of whom had long since "given up their dreams of fame for marriage and domesticity" and were busily "populating Southern California with a younger generation of surprising beauty." New recruits

*Facing page: In the thirties, the Hollywood dream machine fed women's aspirations as never before with a steady stream of glamorous and gutsy female stars. Norma Shearer, for example, had been born to a life of ease in the tony Montreal neighborhood of Westmount. When her father's business failed at the end of the First World War, Norma headed for New York and a career in show business. With little to go on but her success in a beauty contest, she suffered five years of hardship. But by the mid-1930s, she was said to be "Hollywood's richest star," thanks not only to her personal success but also her marriage to studio boss Irving Thalberg.* Photofest/Icon

*Overleaf: And the winner was—no, not Miss Buckeye Lake nor Miss Anthracite. Instead, the judges at the Atlantic City pageant in 1936 gave the crown to Rose Coyle, Miss Philadelphia (back row, seventh from the right) The contest had been revived the year before, after a brief relapse.* Historical Society of Pennsylvania; Princeton Antiques, Atlantic City

INTER CITY BEAUTIES- SHOWMEN'S VARIE

*Atlantic City went movie crazy [in the 1930s] . . . a newspaper account reported that one of the*

*aims of the pageant was to "choose a girl who would 'click' in the movies. . . . in that way, the*

*spectacle may be built into a national institution."*

—Vicky Gold Levi and Lee Eisenberg, in their history of Atlantic City, 1979

*I'm Miss America . . . so what?
They had me posing like I wouldn't
And they photographed me where
they shouldn't
But it's nice to be Miss America,
it makes life so tres gai,
Now if I could only find a way to
eat three times a day*
—sung by Venus Ramey, Miss America 1944, in her night club act

showed up daily to join the "pitiful mobs" that hung around the studios looking for work. Among them were squadrons of beauty queens. Indeed, she observed, "It has become so much the thing for beauty contests, whether organized by municipalities, factories, Rotary Clubs, or newspapers, to send the winner on to Hollywood that the studios have had to develop a technique of discouragement. The applicant is met at the gate of the company affiliated with the contest, rushed through a routine tour of the lot, given a screen test . . . , told she will not do, and bundled onto a plane before she has had time to catch her breath or make arrangements to stay on in the glamour city hoping that her luck will change."

As Thorp is at some pains to point out, Hollywood's glamour was pure fool's gold. If a beauty winner was unlucky enough to stay in town, she would find herself joining the small army of Garbos-in-waiting who earned, on average, just $320 a year, for thirty days' work as extras. These cautionary figures, Thorp suggested, should be "posted annually in all high schools, restaurants, department stores, and beauty parlors" for the edification of star-struck maidens. But there is no indication that young women would have taken kindly to this well-intentioned gesture. For one thing, an extra earned more than a household helper and with much less sweat. For another, as Thorp herself astutely noted, a movie fan looked to Hollywood for temporary relief from her "drab, monotonous, unsatisfying environment": "Better ways of enriching her life, society has not yet taught her." Better ways of enriching her life were often beyond her grasp.

Beauty contests were an adjunct to the Hollywood dream machine, and they should have been one of the thirties' growth industries. If they weren't, it was because of their continuing reputation for scandal and indecency. In 1931, complaints about the "moral dangers" of beauty contests were aired in Geneva before the League of Nations Committee on the Traffic in Women and Children. That same year, the Miss Paris competition ended in turmoil when the winner turned out to be married; a Miss America contest held in Miami had to dump its queen because she was divorced. A hastily convened competition in Atlantic City two years later drew its field of candidates from amusement parks; a rival event in San Diego in 1935 was run by the proprietors of fairground midget and nudie shows. The winner, blonde-and-blue-eyed Florence Cubbitt, was awarded a two-year contract to perform *au naturel*.

At a time when beauty contests should have been making the most of a seller's market in dreams, they seemed intent on burying themselves deeper in sleaze. Somehow or other, they had to reposition themselves. In 1937, the Miss Toronto contest happened upon a way of accomplishing this goal when, after a lapse of several years, the competition was revived as an adjunct to the annual Police Games. As the girls minced around in swimsuits and high heels, the officers exhibited their manliness in athletic events. Later, the local press photographed their queen being tucked into bed by her mom when her day of regal duties was completed.

This squeaky-clean image went down well in Toronto the Good, but it was a little too stodgy for a fun 'n' sun place like Atlantic City. In 1935, when city fathers there decided to reinvent their contest as a headline event, they knew they needed someone to set the right tone. And the someone on whom they pinned their hopes was the honey-voiced, iron-willed Lenora S. Frappart, better known by her maiden name, Miss Slaughter. As a young woman, she had taken a job with the Chamber of Commerce in St. Petersburg, Florida, a position that made her the only female pageant director in the United States. Invited to Atlantic City for a six-week stint in 1935, she would stay for the next thirty-three years, quickly rising through the ranks from assistant to executive secretary to benevolent dictator. With Miss Slaughter's determined assistance, the beauty queen was about to make her big move, up from the gutter and into the middle class.

# Miss America's Makeover

"What I seek above all else is a natural wholesomeness. I do not want types, nor do I want sophistication. I want girls or women who will look like what the advertisers want them to look like, and it is not an easy thing to find." That was how John Robert Powers described the difficulty of locating the right faces for his pioneering modelling agency in New York. And it wasn't a bad description of the challenges that now faced Lenora Slaughter and her beauty contest. Her success depended on coming up with a girl—indeed a long string of girls, year after year—who could create a fresh new image for Atlantic City and its businesses. Times being what they were, she also needed winners who could catch the eye of outside sponsors—the furriers, jewelers, car manufacturers and cosmetics companies to whom, increasingly, she turned for prizes. In return for their generosity, they expected a pretty, smiling, white-skinned girl who would help to push their products.

"Natural wholesomeness"—sex without sleaze—was the key to successful merchandising in the late thirties, and John Robert Powers kept his act clean by discouraging his models from advertising "objectionables," such as undies and swimwear. Poor Lenora Slaughter did not have this luxury; for better or worse, she was stuck with her bathing beauties. "First thing," she said, "I had to get Atlantic City to understand

*By the mid-fifties, the beauty queen had been tamed. These decorous young ladies were enrolled in the Miss Canada pageant for 1956.* Johnny Sharp, *Toronto Telegram,* York University Archives

*Facing page: Rulebook in hand, Lenora Slaughter welcomes three candidates for the title of Miss America 1946. They are (left to right) Georgina Patterson, Timmy Weston and Phyllis Mathis.* Historical Society of Pennsylvania

that it couldn't *just* be a beauty contest." If the event was going to survive, it would have to move significantly upmarket.

Everything Miss Slaughter did served this goal, whether it was changing venues (from the pier to the more dignified precincts of the convention hall), adding a talent competition or enlisting local society matrons to provide one-on-one supervision of the contestants. In keeping with the high tone of the proceedings, these good ladies were referred to as "hostesses" instead of chaperons, and their duties included the enforcement of Miss Slaughter's many new rules. Girls must be in bed by 1 A.M.; they could not smoke or take a drink; they were not to speak to any men during the competition, not even their own fathers. After the disaster of 1937, when the newly crowned Miss America vanished with her official chauffeur, Miss Slaughter wasn't taking any chances with the reputation of her event.

"I tried to make contestants realize it was an honor to be in the Pageant," Miss Slaughter said. She always called it that— "the Pageant"—as if it were a public ceremony instead of a resort contest. Soon the contestants would become "delegates," as the rules were tightened again, this time to ensure that each participant was an accredited representative of her home state. Gone were Miss Bertrand Island, Miss Conshohocken and Miss Anthracite, to be replaced by the likes of Miss Connecticut and Miss Idaho. From 1945 to 1961, the lineup also included Miss Canada, the official representative of what some described as America's unofficial fifty-first state. (An independent Miss Canada contest would not be held until 1963, after a business dispute broke the link with the American contest.)

So much had been accomplished, but Miss Slaughter was not prepared to rest. There were still parents out there who wouldn't allow their daughters to compete; yet these were the very girls the pageant wanted to reach. Who better to lend an aura of middle-class respectability to the proceedings than Middle America's very own daughters? And who better to bring these disbelievers into the fold than the ultra-respectable, ultraright-wing members of the Junior Chamber of Commerce (an organization of businessmen that had chapters throughout Canada and the United States).

I always had trouble with those artists. All they saw was legs and I was a Baptist and my board was Quakers.

—Lenora Slaughter, on her artist judges, 1971

*Facing page: Miss Slaughter had a running battle with the artists who served as judges at the Atlantic City contest. After the talent competition was made compulsory in 1938, the judges were supposed to give it equal weighting with the swimsuit and evening-gown scores. Instead, as one of the artists admitted, they continued to pick "the girl with the best of everything showing." Miss Slaughter, of course, eventually had her way—but not before the judges had chosen Rosemary La Planche, Miss California (second from the right) as the winner for 1941. She went on to star in such blockbuster films as* Strangler of the Swamp.

Historical Society of Pennsylvania

Beginning in 1944 and for decades thereafter, the Jaycees served as front men for Miss Slaughter's shindig by sponsoring the local and state run-ups to the national competition in Atlantic City. In Miss Slaughter's lofty phraseology, "the ideal men of America [were running] a pageant for the ideal women." If anyone still had qualms about impropriety, "we got the local Jaycees to talk to them, and once they understood what we were all about, we got less resistance."

But what really turned the tide for Miss Slaughter's contest were not her alliances, clever as they might be. Instead, unexpectedly, her big break came with the outbreak of war in 1939 and the engagement of the United States in the conflict two years afterward. As the men of the Allied nations were drawn onto the battlefields, women were called up for service in the labor force, where they filled vacated positions or provided much-needed "womanpower" for the production of air-craft, ammunition and other war materiel. In Canada, the number of women with full-time jobs doubled between 1940 and 1945, from 600,000 to 1.2 million. In the United States, total female employment (full- and part-time) grew by a stunning 6 million during those same years. Most startling of all, females were suddenly to be found in distinctly unfeminine jobs, such as carpentry, welding, farm labor and heavy industrial work.

The young factory worker in her dungarees and scarf became the symbol of women's contribution to the war effort. To some, like journalist Lotta Dempsey, she represented "the great and final stage of the movement of women into industry . . . on a complete equality with men." To the Canadian Directorate of Army Recruiting, she stood as a sign of "the complete emancipation of women" that had been achieved during wartime. But others expressed doubts that "equality" and "emancipation" for women were what the world needed most as it descended into the brutality and degradation of total war. Women were still the standard-bear-ers for the good things in life—grace, delicacy, softness, love, home comforts—the very qualities for which Our Brave Boys

*Women's wartime service, both in the military and in industry, gave many people the jitters. Would women who did "men's work" become mannish? Partly to calm these fears, the United States Services created the Miss Armed Forces contest to demonstrate that feminine charm could coexist with khaki.* New York World-Telegram and Sun, *Library of Congress*

*Facing page: In the early forties, Miss Warworker contests were held in Toronto to boost morale among women employed in wartime industries. Instead of bathing suits and evening gowns, the contestants paraded before the judges in their factory garb.* Archives of Ontario

Every war sets women back a generation.

—Pearl S. Buck, 1941

*Facing page: Acknowledging the "morale value" of "eye-arresting pictures" to the fighting men, a Hollywood studio threw a Pinup Party for photographers from the Army, Navy, Marines and Coast Guard. Mary Ann Hyde was one of thirty-four women who had carried the title of Goldwyn Girl.*
Photofest/Icon

were risking their lives. So three cheers for Rosie the Riveter as she marched off to her job, but Heaven forbid that she should lose her womanly charms.

To many people, the wartime mobilization of women was just another sign that the times were desperately out of joint. Women were literally wearing the pants in the domestic workforce and, despite the emergency, it was an alarming sight. In 1942, the Canadian Department of Munitions and Supply attempted to counter these doubts by publishing an appeal for tolerance. Under the headline "Please Don't Stare at My Pants," the ad showed a fur-clad matron glaring disdainfully at a young female war worker dressed in slacks; nearby, a gentleman in white collar and coat smirked at the spectacle. "Would you like to know why I wear trousers like the men when I go about the streets?" the fine print asked. "Because I'm doing a man's job for my country's sake."

"For my country's sake." And when her country no longer needed her, the advertisement seemed to imply, she would happily give up her mannish ways and return to a woman's life. To many people, this thought was the ultimate comfort. As a female war worker was made to say in an ad for Palmolive beauty soap, "I'm a woman in a man's world—But I'm still a woman!" As long as women were women at heart, life would return to normal when the crisis was past. The alternative was so preposterous that it scarcely merited serious thought. Wouldn't it be funny, one journalist asked, if women war workers ultimately "refuse to be stripped of the pants and deprived of the[ir] pay envelopes? What if they start looking round for some nice little chap who can cook and who'll meet them lovingly at the door with their slippers in hand?

# CAMPUS QUEEN

### AYAKO HOSAKA

*Ayako Hosaka was chosen high school queen in an internment camp at Crystal City, Texas, in 1945. Beauty contests were also held in other improbable sites, including Auflag 64, a prisoner-of-war camp in Poland, where a thousand American officers were detained. According to the* New York Times *for November 9, 1944, "The pretty contestants—or reasonable facsimiles of them, by way of photographs—were entered in the contest by the officers, who wrote home for the pictures of their personal 'pin-up girls.' "* Institute of Texan Cultures

What if industry has to organize to give these women sabbatical years for having babies?" These possibilities were enough, she observed, "to make strong men break out in a lather."

Happily, nothing soothes the fears of strong men like the presence of beautiful women. In the context of wartime anxieties, the practice of femininity took on a whole new importance, and women's "beauty" achieved the status of a national resource. "Women in wartime should not relax their efforts to look attractive," wrote a contributor to a British women's magazine. "It is our job to bring colour and cheerfulness to the grim business of war." "You've got to look lovely for his leave," another author urged. "First of all, do eat for beauty. Liver is your meat." And whatever you do, don't let yourself go slack while you are waiting for your man to return. "Have you thought what it will be like if, after the war, men come home to wives and sweethearts who have let themselves go? If you let go now, you may not get the chance to pull up afterwards. Stay lovely."

We will fight on the beaches. We will wear bright-colored lipstick.

Whatever else she might have to offer, "staying lovely" had become every woman's personal and patriotic responsibility. If she was, in the phrase of the Canadian Women's Army Corps newsletter, "the type of gal that sends men swoonin'," she could support the war effort by submitting her photo to the army's pinup contests. If, on the other hand, she was the fresh-faced girl-next-door type, she could be put to work running charitable teas and selling war bonds. If she was a bit of both, like Miss Slaughter's beauty queen, she could fulfill these two functions quite handily. At least, that proved to be true of the eighteen-year-old student from UCLA who was crowned Miss America in the fall of 1942.

Her name was Jean Bartel, and she nurtured a childhood dream of becoming a Broadway star. Yet when, after her win, she was offered $1500 a week to perform at the Roxy Theater in New York, she turned her back on this opportunity. Instead, she decided to stick with the $100-per-week plan devised by Miss Slaughter and duly endorsed by the War Finance Committee of the United States. For fifteen gruelling weeks, Miss America would crisscross the land, singing for the troops, visiting soldiers' hospitals, handing out autographs and raising the profile of her sponsors (Lever Brothers, Butterick Patterns, Tussy Cosmetics, Vimms Vitamins and, of course, the business people of Atlantic City). But her main responsibility would be to sell war bonds to members of service clubs and other audiences.

Admired everywhere she went for her "wholesomeness," Jean Bartel proved to be the best possible advertisement for the war effort. "I never kidded myself," she said afterward. "They were not listening to Jean Bartel, herself, or Jean Bartel, spokeswoman. They were listening to Miss America." One man bought five thousand dollars' worth of bonds in return for a pair of her nylons; another upped the ante to fifty thousand. But most purchases were in small denominations—twenty-five or fifty dollars—and most of the purchasers were women. Traditionally the sharpest critics of beauty contests, middle-class club women now found themselves swayed by Jean Bartel's compelling blend of femininity and patriotism. Thanks to their enthusiastic support, Miss America was able to sell over $1 million of Series E bonds, more than any other individual in the United States.

Back home in Atlantic City after the tour, Miss Slaughter couldn't stop gushing about her girl's success. By remaining "loyal to Atlantic City and the ideals of the Pageant," Jean Bartel had inspired girls everywhere to reach for the "coveted crown" of Miss America. What's more, it was with her help that Miss Slaughter had added the finishing touch to her program. As a coed herself, Jean Bartel had an entrée on campus, and it was during a meeting with the students' council at the University of Minnesota that someone—"an ugly little girl with spectacles" was the only person Miss Slaughter could recall—had come up with the idea of scholarships. Instead of a mink or a Hollywood test, the payoff for her winner henceforth would be a chance to obtain a college degree. Having picked her queen up out of the sand and brought her indoors, Miss Slaughter was preparing to fit her for a mortar board.

*In 1946, Professor Quiz (right) taped an edition of his radio game show,* Battle of Wits, *onstage at the Miss America Pageant. Setting out (he said) to disprove the adage "beautiful but dumb," he proceeded to stump the contestants with rapid-fire trivia questions. But he very nearly met his match in Bess Myerson who, the year before, had become the pageant's first scholarship recipient.* Princeton Antiques, Atlantic City

# There She Is, Your Ideal

𝒯hat first year, 1944, Miss Slaughter raised the impossible sum of five thousand dollars for her scholarship fund. "It was hard, very hard" to find money at a time when all available resources were still supposed to be devoted to the European war, but Miss Slaughter was characteristically single-minded about her goal. "I couldn't [finish] college because of the Depression," she explained. "It was my dream. I wanted it so bad for myself that I tried to see that every girl who wanted to go to college got the chance." (Or every girl who looked good in a bathing suit, at the very least.)

Dreams of one sort and another remained the stock-in-trade of beauty pageants. From the beginning, the contests had offered a playful outlet for the ambitions of young women, and they continued to fulfill this function—albeit with a paradoxical and unplayful earnestness—after the war. As Diane Sawyer (America's Junior Miss for 1963, now the anchor for ABC's flagship news magazine, *Prime Time Live*) once recalled, Miss America "seemed the dreamiest thing to be" in the fifties, and beauty contests mattered in a way they never would again. "I suppose it was because options were so limited then, and [becoming a beauty queen] was the quickest way to vault out of the ordinary."

For young women coming of age in the postwar era, the possibility of leading an extraordinary life—a life of achievement and adventure—was becoming ever more

*How could anything this goofy ever have seemed so normal? As part of the opening festivities at the Miss Universe contest in 1958, Marcia Valisbus, representing the state of Florida, presents two live flamingos to the mayor of Long Beach.* Harry Merrick Studio, Archives of the Historical Society of Long Beach

*Facing page: Girls! Enter! Win! In 1952, when Catalina swimwear launched its Miss Universe contest, the allure of stardom was as bright as ever for many young women.* Courtesy of Authentic Fitness and Miss Universe L.P., LLLP

As the performance of femininity became more engrossing and complex, beauty contests became more fascinating to women and girls. A panel of judges (above) assesses the cake-baking prowess of Sylvia Laherrere in the New Jersey runoff of the Mrs. America contest for 1953. Right, an entrant in a beauty pageant on the Isle of Man enjoys an appreciative audience in the summer of '51. *New York World-Telegram and Sun, Library of Congress; Hulton Getty*

*The ideal fifties woman was wife, mother, hostess, cook, chambermaid, chauffeur and sex goddess, all wrapped into one convenient package.*

## How to Win a Beauty Contest

*There are a few simple tricks that will help you smile more easily on all occasions. The first is to practice smiling when you don't want to. If you are walking down the street, make a game of smiling at lamp posts or at every mailbox you see. . . . Practice your smile at home in front of a mirror until you can feel it starting in your eyes and creeping downward. Try not to show your bottom teeth; they're for eating, not for display.*

*One posing rule is to always bend the leg closest to the camera. And make sure there is no air space between your upper legs if you are wearing a bathing suit.*

*While onstage under hot lights (or parades in hot weather), place a cotton ball or tissue in the cleavage of your bra to absorb perspiration.*

*If you are small-busted or you have wide-set breasts, you can give yourself cleavage without having to have cosmetic surgery. A girl who is an A cup can tape and add silicone implants on the outside for fullness and look like a B or C cup. Never use duct tape or adhesive tape because it will take your skin off.*

—from *How to Win a Beauty Contest*, 1960; *The Beauty Pageant Manual*, 1986; and *101 Secrets to Winning Beauty Pageants*, 1995.

remote. The emancipation that had seemed ripe for the taking thirty years earlier had proven far harder to attain than the flapper generation had imagined. Audacity alone had been no match for the Depression, and sassy gestures of self-assertion had not been encouraged by the exigencies of war. Instead, the crisis had called for teamwork and discipline in both the military and civilian sectors, with clearly defined expectations for both sexes. Men were required for combat; women were called on to provide support services in the armed forces, in war industries and in the home. Excluded (for better or worse) from the real business of war, women were to serve as ever-smiling, sweet 'n' sexy helpmates for the boys.

This powerful consensus about women's supportive role translated effortlessly into the period of peace and reconstruction that followed. Normalcy had been reestablished, at a terrible cost, and normalcy implied homes and children. Women who had sustained their households financially during the war were advised to quit their jobs in order to protect the frail egos of their returning menfolk. Those who failed to do so were often unceremoniously dumped to free up positions for the veterans. (In the United States, for example, one-quarter of female factory workers lost their jobs within weeks of the armistice.) Excluded anew from the best-paying jobs, women were to return to their homes and serve as ever-smiling, sweet 'n' sexy wives and mothers.

A few years down the road, some of these same women would get a little tetchy about their exile among the neatly clipped hedges and lawns of suburbia, but at the time, many of them settled into domestic life with every appearance of contentment. Miss America 1947, Barbara Jo Walker, spoke for thousands when, turning her back on a movie deal, she proclaimed that the only contract that interested her was a marriage contract. More women were getting married, at younger ages, than at any time in recent history, and sales of cribs, carriages and Dr. Spock's *Baby and Child Care* soared, in sync with a dramatic and persistent rise in the birth rate. This "baby boom" (which, with its echoes, continues to reverberate through the economy) retained its full force until the late 1950s, when a decade of dirty diapers and midnight feedings finally began to dampen the postwar enthusiasm for child rearing.

Even with the assistance of "labor-savers" like cake mixes, pop-up toasters and clothes dryers (among many other marvels of postwar technology), women had their hands full—and not just with their domestic duties. Increasingly, they were also going out to work to supplement the family earnings. Expelled from heavy industry after the war, they had quietly returned to their familiar employments in shops, offices, schools and other suitably feminine sites of labor. Between 1940 and 1960, the percentage of women who worked for pay doubled in the United States and, in keeping with the long-term trend, a majority of the new recruits were married. But, as ever, the jobs open to women offered low status, miserable remuneration and little hope of getting ahead. To make a bad situation worse, many wives were now juggling the demands of home and career by working part-time or dropping out of the labor force for long periods to raise their children.

A truly good woman would never dream of pursuing a serious career and, thus, had no real need for a college education. Schooling was a pleasant refinement for a wife, one that equipped her to make intelligent conversation with her husband, but most people agreed that it was not essential for a woman's success. Although girls continued to graduate from high school in large numbers, they were becoming a rare breed at American colleges and universities (and this despite Miss Slaughter's efforts

> Don't do your housework in a trailing negligee and scuffs. . . . Comfortable and appropriate clothes . . . speed the work along and make you feel well-dressed while you are doing it. Put on some lipstick too, and then you are ready to answer the door with confidence.
>
> —Marguerite Dodd,
> *America's Homemaking Book*
> 1957

*The high-voltage smiles of these Santa Monica bathing beauties outshine even the hot summer sun. Incidentally, the bikini swimsuit (named after a nuclear bomb blast on the Bikini Atoll) was first seen in competition at the Miss World contest in London in 1951, where it aroused such a firestorm of protest that it was subsequently banned.* Del Hagen Studio, Santa Monica Public Library Archives

The flush of prosperity that followed the Second World War was the long-delayed answer to the ad men's prayers. Though times had changed, the key to successful marketing remained the same. An eye-catching array of half-clad "beauties" could be used to sell anything, from a good spinal alignment to antifreeze and the underwater shows at Weeki Wachee Springs. UPI/Corbis-Bettmann (right and far right); Photo Communications, *New York World-Telegram and Sun*, Library of Congress (below)

*The first duty of a woman is to attract. . . .*
*It does not matter how clever or independent you*
*may be, if you fail to influence the men you meet,*
*consciously or unconsciously, you are not fulfilling*
*your fundamental duty as a woman.*

—Advertising copy, early 1900s

to the contrary). From a high of almost 50 percent in the 1920s, the proportion of young women on American campuses had fallen to 35 percent by 1958. Of these students, the majority were studying for secretarial, nursing, home economics or teaching certificates. Medical and law schools maintained tight quotas of 5 percent or less for female admissions, and the proportion of women receiving PhDs had fallen below one in ten for the first time since 1910.

In Canada, where overall female enrollments had always been lower than in the United States, women's participation in undergraduate programs sagged after the war and then crept up, until by 1960, "co-eds" made up a meager one-quarter of the student population. Meanwhile, women's admission to postgraduate studies had plummeted through the Depression and the war, to bottom out at about 14 percent by the end of the fifties. Why would a woman go to the trouble of getting an MSc, when the distinction she really needed was a simple Mrs.?

And even when it came to attaining this cherished goal, a girl was tightly hemmed in. No matter how much she might like a young man, she couldn't call him up or ask him for a date; nor would she ever dream of proposing marriage. Those were all the guy's prerogatives. The girl's role was to stand around in her poodle skirt and wait for the phone to ring. Her other essential task, of course, was to guard her virginity. Although everybody now expected young people to "neck" and "pet" (a sweaty and frustrating struggle in the back seat of the family Buick), it was still up to the girl to set the limits. "We'd be inches away from doing it," one woman recalled, "and [my boyfriend] would be moaning, 'Oh baby, baby, baby!' and I'd be moaning, 'No, no, no. . . .' Oh, it was complicated."

With her sexuality and ambitions censored and controlled, a young woman was walled in like Rapunzel in her tower. The only approved way to survive this confinement was through the practices of beauty. In the foreword to a 430-page beauty course

> The whole Pageant was set up to convince us that we had to behave like ladies. It was like a coming-out party. . . . Then when you had finally become one of the debutantes, what did they want? They wanted you to smile and wink and pull your skirt higher and sell hair tonic for them. . . .
>
> —Bess Myerson, Miss America 1945

*Facing page: Four beauty queens from Canada step off the plane in New York, ready to do whatever it takes to get the attention of the media. Here, in their gloves and pearls, are Miss Canada, Dalyce Smith; Miss By-Line, Ivi Riives; Miss Photo Queen, Pamela D'Orsay; and Miss Toronto, Sheila Billing.*
Photofest/Icon

FEBRUARY 1955

# PHOTOPLAY

THE WORLD'S TOP
FILM MAGAZINE

1'3

Ruth Hampton--
big break for
a beauty queen

published in the late forties (and into its twelfth printing by 1953), a Dr. C. C. Crawford, Professor of Education, explained that the purpose of beauty culture was "to make women more interesting, attractive and skilful in their personal contacts." This, the good doctor asserted, was the feminine road to fulfillment. "Whether in the office or in the drawing-room, or even across the breakfast table, appearance and behaviour make the difference between success and failure." It was by applying the "60 Easy Ways to Beautify and Improve Your Figure," the "Thirty Exciting, New, Easily-Applied Makeup Tricks," the "Unique, How to Dress-at-a-Glance Chart," and the "Quick Ways to Improve Your Hair, Face, Hands, Figure, Legs, Voice, Etc.," that women could trade the prospect of poverty, spinsterhood or divorce for an assurance of wealth, marriage and wedded bliss. Although the work of beauty might seem trivial in itself, the results, as the professor averred, were far from trifles.

> The boys in my neighbourhood hoped to get out of a lifetime in the factories through sports; the girls, if we imagined anything other than marrying a few steps up in the world, always dreamed of show-business careers.
>
> —Gloria Steinem, 1984

Simply by learning how to hold her head quietly, stand up gracefully and make pleasant small talk, a young woman could transform herself "into the person [she wanted] to be." She could take charge of her life; or at least, that was the promise. "Be the Best You Can Be." "Become the Self of Your Dreams." An infinite world of possibilities seemed to open up through the practice of charm and beauty. In steadfast denial of the actual restrictions on women's options, beauty courses—and beauty contests—were sold as a vehicle for self-improvement through which women and girls could attain success and happiness. In Canada and the United States, beauty pageants became "finishing schools" for middle-class girls who, in the run-up to the judging, received training in makeup, etiquette and general deportment. It got to the point where one contestant complained that picking up the wrong fork to eat her smoked salmon at lunch would probably ruin her chances in the competition.

In England, where a new and vigorous system of contests had developed after the war (under the auspices of Mecca, a company that ran a chain of dance halls), the appeal to self-improvement was also powerful. Girls were drawn to any contest that promised

*Although women were urged to devote themselves to enhancing their looks, they were also expected to stay within decent limits. Too much makeup made a girl look like a tart. And as for wearing falsies—unthinkable! When Wendy Peters was crowned Miss England for 1958, she felt the wrath of the losers' moms, who were scandalized by rumors that she had worn a girdle. UPI/ New York World-Telegram and Sun, Library of Congress*

*Facing page: Ruth Hampton's big break consisted of nothing more than a month's exposure on the newsstands.*

*Facing page: The Holiday Girl Beauty Contest, organized by Butlin's vacation camps in England, gave young women a chance to put on some class. Here, amid a froth of chiffon, a contestant named Judy Dunlop uses the King's library at Brighton to make last-minute adjustments, 1953.* Hulton Getty

them a chance to spruce up on "their poise, dress-sense and make-up." By the early sixties, this pitch was attracting sufficient entrants to fill the rosters of eight major competitions (Miss England, Miss Britain, and two each of Miss Scotland, Miss Ireland and Miss Wales), plus countless local heats. Regional winners went on to compete in glitzy international events, such as Miss World (initiated by Mecca in 1951), Miss Universe (an American contest first held a year later, in conjunction with Miss U.S.A., its sister event) and Miss International Beauty (a rival of Miss Universe). By the end of the decade, Miss World had drawn its queens from such far-flung territories as Sweden, Egypt, Venezuela and white South Africa.

As beauty contests enlarged their reach around the world, they also began to diversify into new demographic markets. In the United States, for example, a cradle-to-grave-system of pageants began to develop, with the introduction of Mrs. America, for married women, in 1938; the National College Queen, for coeds, in 1955; and America's Junior Miss, for teenyboppers, three years afterward. If attracting and keeping a man was a woman's lifelong goal, there were no age limits on the quest to be beautiful. Beauty—the complex skills that a woman required to be an interesting companion, stylish consumer, gracious hostess and bedtime playmate for her personal leading man—was the one true vocation of a human female.

In 1954, when the Miss America Pageant made its debut on network television, it carried this message to almost 30 million Americans, and most of the people who tuned in to watch were girls and women. As the "Superbowl of Femininity," Miss America would continue to top the TV ratings throughout the sixties, ranking as the first or second most popular show eight years out of ten and attracting a mass audience of armchair participants. Soon, a dozen similar events would crowd onto the screen, including the Miss World contest on the BBC. "They hadn't burned their bras yet and there was still some hero worship left," one fifties winner observed. It really was "an ideal time" for the whole beauty business.

> The first thing I am going to do with the money is to find a nice flat. I live in Bayswater in a bed sitter with a kitchen.
>
> —Lesley Langley, Miss World 1965

# Black and White

Culturally speaking, the fifties lasted well into the next decade—until the very time, in fact, when an aging Miss Slaughter was preparing to leave her post at Miss America. As she approached her retirement in 1967, she could look back with pride on the "reputation and stability" that she had brought not only to her own event but to beauty pageants as a whole. Under her guidance, the schizy, scandalous bathing beauty of the twenties (part jazz baby, part mother of the nation) had developed a stable identity as "the ideal American girl." Even people who had felt the sting of Miss Slaughter's disapproval, like Bess Myerson, Miss America 1945—the first and only Jewish girl to don the royal robes—were generous in their assessment of her accomplishments.

"I was always impressed by her ability to sell," Myerson said. "Those she couldn't convince, she charmed; those she couldn't charm, she simply outlasted. I watched her feed her 'dreams and ideals' pitch to hundreds and hundreds of people and make them believe it as I believed it. Truthfully, I have never stopped believing it. In all these years, I have never stopped believing that great good could be achieved through the instrument of the Miss America Pageant."

One of the most impressive tributes to Miss Slaughter's achievements—if she'd had the grace to see it—came from a group of people who were also her fiercest detractors. Persuaded, like Bess Myerson, that great good could be achieved through

*When Bess Myerson was chosen as Miss America 1945, Lenora Slaughter suggested she change her name to disguise the fact that she was Jewish. Not only did Myerson refuse, she went on to use her position as national "queen" to oppose bigotry. "You can't be beautiful and hate," she told her audiences. Princeton Antiques, Atlantic City*

*Facing page: In 1955, African American women arrived in New York to compete for the "coveted title" of Miss United States. Jeanne Owens, Miss Virginia, was among the lineup of contestants. Photofest/Icon*

*Sponsored by the National Association for the Advancement of Colored People, the Miss Black America contest ran head to head with Miss [White] America in 1968 in what was described by organizers as a "positive protest." "The beauty of the black woman has been ignored."* Archive Photos

the pageant, African Americans had, by the mid-sixties, begun to protest their exclusion from the Miss America extravaganza. Although segregated beauty contests had for years been run by magazines and organizations that served the black community, high-profile pageants had remained the privileged domain of pale-skinned maidens. In the almost fifty-year history of Miss America, only one Native American had ever made it into the competition at Atlantic City—Mifaunwy Shunatona, Miss Oklahoma for 1941. Irma Nydia Vasquez, a young woman of Hispanic ancestry from Puerto Rico, and Yun Tau Zane, the first Asian contestant, as Miss Hawaii, had broken the color bar again in 1948, but no African American had ever been admitted to the parade of states. Whenever the issue was raised, Miss Slaughter would point to Rule Seven in some tattered copy of the Miss America handbook: "Contestants must be of good health and of the white race."

But the times they were a-changin', however glacially. In 1954, *Ebony* magazine announced a major breakthrough—"Jamaican girl is the first Negro to enter top beauty contest." Evelyn Andrade (identified as "white" in her homeland because her father was Syrian) looked black to *Ebony* by virtue of her "colored" mother, and her claims on the title of Miss Universe were celebrated in four lavish pages of color photographs. It would be another six years before the first black American reached a national beauty final—Corinne Hunt, Miss Ohio for 1960—and again it was in the Miss U.S.A./Miss Universe system. Finally, in 1968, Valerie Dickinson proved that "Black is Beautiful," when she was crowned National College Queen on network television. But the Miss America Pageant, the most prestigious of the lot, remained a complete whiteout.

Thus it was that in the fall of that same year—on the very day when Miss America was being selected in the Atlantic City Convention Hall—the first Miss Black America Pageant was held a few blocks away. As one of the (male) organizers explained, "There's a need for the beauty of the black woman to be paraded and applauded as a symbol of universal pride." But for the winner, an eighteen-year-old college student named Saundra Williams, the issues were more visceral. "With my title, I can show black women that they, too, are beautiful. We keep saying that over and over because for so long none of us believed it, but now we're finally coming around."

A few years earlier, when reporters had pressed a newly crowned Miss [white] America for her views on beauty's apartheid system, her handlers had refused to let her reply. "She shouldn't have to answer a question about a national problem," Miss Slaughter had hissed, as she whisked the girl out of the room. "She's not the President." But the pageant itself clearly had to respond to the growing chorus of criticism. It did so by working with the NAACP to encourage "Negro beauties" to come forth and by appointing a small number of African Americans as chaperons and board members. In 1969, the board appointed its first black judge, Dr. Zelma

> I see my appointment as a dramatization of all those who have been left out before: Indians, Cuban-Americans, Puerto Ricans, Negroes.
>
> —Dr. Zelma George, from a report in the *New York Times,* 1969

*Crowning a queen was an all-purpose response to minority issues in the fifties and sixties. Any group that felt the need to assert its existence—from the Saskatchewan Farmers Union to the Sephardic Jews of Los Angeles—might throw the mantle of group identity onto the shoulders of a young girl. Lynn Lam, for example, carried the pride of Vancouver's Chinese neighborhoods when she stood as a candidate for Chinatown's Centennial Queen, about 1960. National Archives of Canada*

*In 1970, the Virgin Islands Public Affairs Council crowned its beauty winner in the bright lights of New York. For an "emerging" nation, beauty contests offer a way of attracting media attention that helps to put the country on the map.* Schomburg Center for Research in Black Culture, Austin Hansen Collection

George, director of the Cleveland Job Corps for Women, who said she had accepted the invitation after assuring herself that the pageant was not a skin show but an adjudication of "the personality, taste and intelligence" of young women. The first African American contestant arrived in Atlantic City the very next year—twenty-year-old Cheryl Browne of Iowa. Despite her doll-like features and cascades of long, straight hair, Browne failed to place among the ten finalists, though she was awarded a scholarship for her talent.

One of the people who cheered these reforms from a distance was a disaffected former Miss America (and Miss Alabama) named Yolande Betbeze. As feisty and outspoken as she was exotically named, the lovely Miss Betbeze had strong opinions and a good loud voice (before her marriage to millionaire Matthew Fox, she had been studying for a career in the opera house). Ever since her reign in 1951, she had used her full vocal powers to condemn the pageant for its exclusion of black women. "Pageant officials weren't very happy about it," she admitted, "but I had to speak out." And she didn't get any more popular when she opened her mouth again to itemize the other reforms that she thought beauty contests should make.

From the beginning, Yolande Betbeze had been (to use Miss Slaughter's word) kind of "ornery." Within days of her coronation, she had made it clear that she would not pose in a bathing suit when she went on tour. She was an opera singer, not a porn queen, and displaying herself half-naked was an affront to her dignity. Miss Slaughter had to agree. The result was an awkward dispute with one of the pageant's sponsors, the makers of Catalina swimwear, who eventually went off in a huff and organized their own

competitions. If Miss America had become too nicey-nice to model bathing suits, then Miss U.S.A. and Miss Universe would be only too happy to do it.

The new competitions were to emphasize "beauty," pure and simple, with none of the ridiculous folderol about talent and scholarships. Just a lineup of eye-catching girls in eye-catching fashions. But even with this objective clearly in sight, the organizers found they had to make concessions to higher values. By 1959, the Catholic church had renewed its ban on beauty contests, and Catholic contestants now faced the threat of being expelled from church-run schools or denied the sacraments. The church's objection, as ever, was to the bathing-suit parade, which was seen as posing a dire threat to the family. The Miss Universe contest, for its part, saw only a threat to itself, since it drew many of its participants from Catholic parts of the world. "We maintain the contest on a very high moral level," the director wearily explained. As evidence, he adduced the fact that the contestants all had to give little talks on "bringing more understanding among countries of the world. I think this pageant helps do that, don't you?"

But no matter how hard the pageants tried to change the subject, the debate kept coming back to the same old riveting preoccupation—sex. Alfred Kinsey's report on *Sexual Behavior in the Human Female,* published in 1953, had made it official that women experience the same range of sexual passions and responses as men do. But the critical question remained: what were women supposed to do with their newly acknowledged and documented sexuality? What were female bodies *for*? Was the Catholic church right to insist that they were meant for producing children within the holy estate of marriage? Or was Hugh Hefner on the mark when in the inaugural issue of *Playboy* magazine (also published in 1953), he championed sexual self-expression and pleasure? And who should be pleasing whom?

I'm just sick. I've trained her for so long.

—Mrs. Edward Belitz, commenting on the withdrawal of her daughter Mary Jean from the Miss America pageant, under threat of expulsion from her Catholic college, *New York Times,* 1959

*Representatives from fifteen countries, including India (fourth from left) and Turkey (second from right) do their bit for international understanding by displaying their national dress. In all the peace and goodwill, no one objected to the presence of a white delegate from South Africa (far right), a frequent cause of dissent at other international pageants. The first nonwhite Miss South Africa, Palesa Jacqui Mofokeng, was named in 1993.* Archives of the Historical Society of Long Beach

*Facing page: Less fastidious about her dignity than was Yolande Betbeze, Christine Martel celebrates her victory as Miss Universe 1954 by posing in her swimwear.* Perry Griffith Photographers, Photofest/ Icon

*Getting into the spirit of the event, a photographer works with contestants in the Miss Nude World Pageant in 1971.* Brian Willer, *Toronto Telegram*, York University Archives

*Playboy* urged its male readers to use women to meet their own needs—"to enjoy the pleasures the female has to offer without becoming emotionally involved." Hefner profited handsomely from this philosophy, amassing a personal fortune that was estimated at $100 million by the mid-1960s. The circulation of his magazine with its naked centerfolds—known, like beauty queens, as Miss January or Miss July—peaked at 6 million by the end of the decade, when it began to lose market share to more aggressive pornography.

The *Playboy* centerfold was, as much as anything, the poster girl for a new, more overtly sexual approach to marketing that now extended far beyond the covers of so-called "adult" magazines. From 1949 on, a brassiere company had sent its cone-cupped model into public view as she explored a rich dream life in the semi-nude: "I Dreamed I Stopped Traffic in my Maidenform Bra." Meanwhile, Revlon played with the sexual thermostat in a steamy "Fire and Ice" promotion for its lipstick and nail polish. "Does she or doesn't she?" teased the headline on ads for Clairol hair coloring, with a wink and a nudge of sexual double-meaning.

The sexual sell was, and is, the most basic technique of modern advertising. Ever since Henry Ford turned the switch on his first assembly line, the challenge has been to keep it going—to promote a pace of consumption that can meet the demands of mass production. Stimulating consumer demand is the task of advertising, and it does this (as it has always done) by fanning the fires of pleasure and self-indulgence. Our whole commercial system runs on *desire*. In the powerful visual language of advertising culture, beautiful young women had become a metaphor for everything and anything that could be construed as desirable. The nascent trend that Raymonde Allain and Mae West had sensed back in the twenties toward using women as "lighted signs" for commercial purposes blazed from the billboards, magazines and television screens of the fifties and sixties.

"The basis for any industry that needs immediate attention of the public . . . today is . . . the exploitation of the female form." Mae West had written that in 1927, though she was not unduly upset by what she observed. "I happen to be smart enough to play

Posing for those pictures bothered me, but I wasn't strong enough or assertive enough then to say what I really felt. That's not just a life lesson, that's a *woman's* lesson: learning that you don't have to please everyone.

—Vanessa Williams, 1997

it their way," her movie persona growled. But, by the mid- to late 1960s, a growing number of women were starting to fear that this was a hollow boast. If the purpose of a woman was to fulfill her own desires, she didn't need cosmetics companies, women's magazines and beauty-contest impresarios telling her what to do, what to want and what to buy. What she needed instead, as Raymonde Allain had so astutely pointed out, was to be left alone with the hope of becoming herself.

In the consumer orgy of the sixties, this was a radical complaint, and one of the women who voiced it was the "ornery" and determined Yolande Betbeze. And so it was that in September of 1968—just as Miss Black America was being crowned and paraded through town—Betbeze took part in the rowdy "Women's Lib" demonstration outside the Atlantic City Convention Hall. As the protesters danced and chanted, they too denounced the Miss America Pageant for its racism. But their main objective was to decry the confining and demeaning roles that were forced upon all women. "Basically, we're against all beauty contests," Robin Morgan said, in her role as spokesperson for the demonstrators. "We deplore Miss Black America as much as Miss White America but we understand the black issue involved."

Whether or not sixties feminists fully understood black issues is a moot point. Perhaps not. But they were nonetheless right to suggest that black women suffered at least as much as anyone else from commercial exploitation. If that hadn't been clear before, it became unavoidably obvious in 1984 when Vanessa Williams—the first African American to wear the Miss America crown—was forced to resign partway through her year. As a teenager, Williams had let herself be pressured into posing for porn photos, on the understanding that they would never appear in print. But in July of 1984, the pictures were published in all their naughty splendor in *Penthouse* magazine, where they netted publisher Bob Guccione a windfall profit of $14 million.

*After Vanessa Williams's resignation, her place was filled by runner-up Suzette Charles, seen here clowning for a hometown crowd in Mays Landing, New Jersey. As for Williams, she took her lumps with grace and has since enjoyed notable success as a singer and actress.* Donna Connor/Princeton Antiques, Atlantic City

# The Show Must Go On

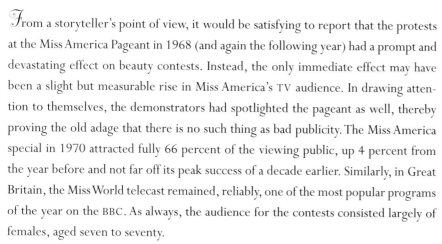

From a storyteller's point of view, it would be satisfying to report that the protests at the Miss America Pageant in 1968 (and again the following year) had a prompt and devastating effect on beauty contests. Instead, the only immediate effect may have been a slight but measurable rise in Miss America's TV audience. In drawing attention to themselves, the demonstrators had spotlighted the pageant as well, thereby proving the old adage that there is no such thing as bad publicity. The Miss America special in 1970 attracted fully 66 percent of the viewing public, up 4 percent from the year before and not far off its peak success of a decade earlier. Similarly, in Great Britain, the Miss World telecast remained, reliably, one of the most popular programs of the year on the BBC. As always, the audience for the contests consisted largely of females, aged seven to seventy.

"We only allow our two girls to stay up late to watch TV for one program," President Richard Nixon confided in 1972, voicing the public mood. That one program, inevitably, was the Miss America finals.

Meanwhile, women's liberationists were staying up nights as well, trying to think of new ways to discredit the contests and dislodge them from their privileged place at the heart of popular culture. "The feminists were so rampant," a seventies queen complained. "They would start literally bra burning in front of my motorcades and

*Kimberley Aiken, the fifth black woman to reign as Miss America, bestows the honor on her successor, Heather Whitestone—Miss America 1994—who is hearing impaired and is the first disabled person to win a national crown. Updated for the nineties, the Miss America program prides itself on honoring women's achievements and diversity. Yet at the same time, it enforces a standard of physical beauty that has become ever more narrowly defined in recent decades. UPI/Corbis-Bettmann*

*Facing page: Beauty contests have gone global in the nineties, but some things never change. Here, in a broadcast from Manila, Miss India, Sushmita Sen, reacts with gape-mouthed surprise as she is named Miss Universe for 1994, while her closest rival, Carolina Gomez, simulates delight at being defeated. UPI/Corbis-Bettmann*

burning me in effigy. It wasn't *me* [that they were attacking]. It was what I was representing. . . . But I took it very personally, and it was scary!!" It was also, as political protests go, remarkably ineffective. For the better part of a decade, the ratings for the contests did not budge. And then, suddenly, in 1977, for no discernible outward cause, Miss America and Miss Universe both took a fall.

For Miss America in particular, it was the beginning of a downward trend that would cut her audience in half by 1984. (Thus, by the time the pageant crowned Vanessa Williams, Miss America herself was something of a has-been.) Part of this decline was almost certainly the long-delayed effect of more than a decade of feminist critique. "There was a new me inside my head," said one convert to the cause, and thousands of "new mes" around the land found themselves offended by what now could be discerned as the banality and tawdriness of beauty competitions. But other women defected on more conventional grounds. Miss America, they charged, had let herself get run-down.

This problem actually dated back to the end of Miss Slaughter's reign and her insistence on imposing the fashion sense of a bygone day. Having devoted her adult life to imbuing the pageant with taste, she was not about to see her girls flashing around in bikinis, miniskirts and other excesses of the modern age. If she had anything to do with it (which, of course, she did), the contestants would attire themselves with appropriate dignity, in one-piece panel swimsuits and hems that reached the knee. It didn't matter to her if such apparel could not be

I believe these contests no longer merit national airtime. They are an anachronism in this day and age of equality, and verging on the offensive.

—BBC spokesman Michael Grade, on the decision to suspend the annual Miss World broadcast, 1984

found in the stores. She had the reputation of her pageant to uphold, and so did her successor, who closely followed her lead. But Miss America's lack of razzmatazz mattered a great deal to the women and girls out in TV land. To them, the much-vaunted "queen of femininity" had become the queen of dowdiness. Miss America had all the star quality of a corn-fed hick who dressed herself off the bargain racks at the local Kresge's.

Margaret Gorman—the very first Miss America, back in 1921—summed up the situation with admirable directness. "They don't give a damn about her in the big cities any more," she observed. "The girl only goes over in the podunk towns." Unable to command the attention of urbanites or of the crucial eighteen-to-forty-five-year-old sector of the female population (the group of most interest to advertisers), Miss America was soon on the outs with her sponsors as well. As she approached her sixty-fifth year, she, like many another aging beauty, seemed to be fading into oblivion.

Women's lives had changed in fundamental ways since Miss America was a kid. Back then, entering a beauty contest had been a gesture of defiance against the lingering clouds of Victorian prudishness. By parading around in full public view in their daring bathing costumes, a generation of saucy young women had done their best to let the sunshine in. However coyly and tentatively, they had lifted up the veil that impeded their movements and obscured their desires. As one contemporary commentator quipped, the clock had suddenly struck "sex" in America. But the bells that chimed for pleasure also rang out for wedded bliss, since everyone agreed that sexuality must be expressed only within marriage. Although girls might work at dead-end jobs for a while after leaving school, the natural career of a woman was family and home. It had been a childish daydream to hope for anything more.

A lifetime later, as the women of the twenties entered their declining years, daydreams were becoming realities for their granddaughters and great-granddaughters. Women were on the move. After a half century in the doldrums, female enrollments at universities were on a steady rise. What's more, thanks to persistent pressure from the women's movement, the quotas on admissions to law and medical schools had finally been outlawed, and the proportion of women in professional colleges had increased tenfold. Although many women were still trapped in boring, badly paid jobs, most had at least escaped the confines of their homes. By the mid-eighties, almost

*Facing page: In an effort to "give the girls a break"—and grab some media attention with a new face—Palisades Amusement Park crowned a king instead of a queen in 1953. The winner, Pat Moore, is seen here getting the once-over from other members of the park's "royal family" of beauty.*

*Though the photo tries to insist that this king is a girl-pleaser, the main audience for pictures of good-looking guys was actually gay men. With the proliferation of novelty titles and the emergence of "alternative" audiences, beauty contests began to lose their straightforward focus on feminine perfection. And when the drag queen burst out of the closet with her parody of the whole scene, beauty contests became very difficult to take seriously.* Bert Nevins, Inc., *New York World-Telegram and Sun,* Library of Congress

*In 1985, activist Ann Simonton was arrested for incitement to riot (not just misbehavin'), after she and a fellow protester splashed their own blood on the sidewalk outside the Miss California Pageant. "Every man who enters this auditorium walks on the blood of raped women," they warned those who approached.*

*A former beauty queen and cover girl, Simonton was gang-raped on her way to a modeling job in the early seventies. In time, she began to sense a connection between the seductive, depersonalized depiction of women in the media (in which she was participating) and the violence she had suffered. Since then, resistance to the media's depiction of women, in beauty contests and other forms, has become her life's work. She is a founder and director of MediaWatch, a nonprofit organization based in Santa Cruz, California.* AP/Wide World Photos

two-thirds of American women were employed (through both necessity and desire), including a majority of those who were also mothers and wives. More and more, the career paths of women resembled those of men. In millions of homes in the western world—if sometimes under duress—husbands were changing diapers, sorting dirty clothes and doing the dishes.

As to sex, there was no longer any great need to assert that women were interested. The word blared from the cover of every women's magazine, from racy *Cosmopolitan* to homey *McCall's*. And women's bodies, once so shameful and unseen, were now freely exposed from every conceivable angle in advertising, movies and drugstore pornography. If anything, what was needed now was not more exposure but more restraint. The female body was on constant display as an all-purpose sign of desire. Instantly recognizable, infinitely repeatable, it served as an emblem of lust for cars, cosmetics, clothes and an endless variety of other consumer goods. How was a woman to free herself from this tumult of images? How was she to acknowledge her self and her desires in their full humanness?

Clearly, if the people at Miss America hoped to bring their program into the 1990s, they would have to do more than give their girl a fresh coat of glitter and style. They were going to have to acknowledge, however belatedly, the possibilities and perplexities of a new generation of young women. To this end, in the late 1980s, the pageant arose from its own ashes as the Miss America Organization, an umbrella structure that not only runs the beauty show but also raises scholarship prizes for contestants and, in a smaller way, supports the university careers of other female

students. No longer willing to be thought of as a beauty contest, the Miss America group now advertises itself as the world's largest scholarship fund for women. With total disbursements in excess of $32 million per year, this may well be an accurate boast.

In keeping with its new emphasis on career preparation and community involvement, the pageant requires its winner to identify herself with a social issue or platform that she will promote during her reign. For example, Leanza Cornett, Miss America 1993, chose the unladylike subject of AIDS prevention. But if the beauty queen now has serious work to do, she still has to worry about looking good in a bathing suit. Although the bathing-beauty parade at Miss America is now called "Fitness in Swimsuit," it is really just the same old display of female flesh on the hoof. "I used to tell everyone, 'It's not a beauty pageant. It's not a beauty pageant,'" the forthright Ms. Cornett says. "But hey—if it looks like a duck and walks like a duck, it *is* a duck"—so there.

The Miss Universe contest, by contrast, has never seriously claimed to be anything else. It is a glamorous duck and proud of it. Less popular than Miss America in the fifties and sixties, it didn't have as far to fall when the downturn came in the late seventies. Not only did it quickly rebound to its previous ratings, it also kept hold of the crucial eighteen-to-forty-five demographic. Rather than make concessions to feminist demands, the men who run Miss Universe kept on doing what they do so well—displaying the charms of pretty girls from a succession of exotic locales. In 1996, under the co-ownership of Donald Trump, the Miss Universe contest was seen by an estimated 600 million people in sixty countries around the world.

The developing world is the growth market for beauty contests. For a country like Nicaragua or the British Virgin Islands (still struggling to assert an independent identity in the wake of colonialism), a beauty queen can provide a focus for national

Calling the Miss America Pageant a scholarship competition is like calling *Wheel of Fortune* a road race just because they give away a car at the end.

—Michelle Anderson, Miss Santa Cruz 1988, who disrupted the Miss California Pageant by unfurling a banner that read "Pageants Hurt All Women"

*Preparations for the staging of the British-based Miss World contest in Bangalore, India, aroused a storm of protest in 1996. Here, people dressed as figures from Hindu mythology display a cutout of the contest producer, Indian actor Amitabh Bachchan, exposed for all the world to see. The protest brought together unlikely allies, including religious groups (to whom the contest was indecent), nationalist parties (who objected to the cultural intrusion) and feminist groups (who were alarmed, as ever, by the shallow, eroticized "ideal" that was being promoted). In the end, the contest went ahead, though the swimsuit competition was shunted to the Seychelles. AP/Wide World Photos*

*Facing page: Shawn Nichols Weatherly, Miss USA 1980, and Maritza Sayalero, Miss Universe '79, both bear the trademark "look" of the Miss Universe organization, which owns and administers both titles. Photofest/Icon*

*"A woman's body should be whatever she wants it to be."*

*That is Laurie Fierstein's credo, one that has made her among the strongest and most muscular women in the world. Winner of the Ms. USA Bodybuilding Championship in 1991, she can lift 435 pounds (more than three times her own competition weight), yet she is only 4' 10" tall.*

*Fierstein describes herself as a "walking rebellion" against the ingrained idea that women should be weak and defenseless. No longer comfortable in the competitive realm (where hypermuscular women are seen to have gone "too far"), she now pursues bodybuilding as a work of art. For her, the desire to shape and display her body represents a woman's yearning to exist as her own true self and to make that self visible.* Photo by Mark Schaeffer, courtesy of Laurie Fierstein

togetherness. A girl who does her country proud by winning at Miss Universe or Miss World is accorded the full honors of a national hero. The international success of a Miss Thailand or a Miss Venezuela or a Miss Jamaica is headline news for days, and everybody tunes in to watch her homecoming. There are presidential parties, parades, commemorative stamps and, on the business page, a lot of happy chatter about the benefits of her victory for the tourist trade. The more things change, as Raymonde Allain might have said, the more they stay the same.

As always, beauty contests continue to serve complex national, social and commercial purposes. And just as in the past, the contestants are used to promote these interests. Yet every year, thousands of young women continue to try their luck, whether in Saskatoon, Saskatchewan (home of the "Pizzazz Model Search"); Ho Chi Minh City, Vietnam (where all beauty contestants must be medically certified virgins); or Jinan, Shandong Province (proud host of the "China Supermodel of the Year" competition). And everywhere, young women enter beauty contests, as they have always done, for what seem at the time to be very good reasons. They come looking for excitement, prizes, experience or escape—a chance to break away from the common herd and become the next Oprah, Cindy, Naomi or Kate. They want to get on with their lives.

In 1968, before the Miss America protest, the members of New York Radical Women set out their basic beliefs. First and foremost on the list was a commitment to "take the woman's side in everything. We ask not if something is 'reformist,' 'radical,' 'revolutionary,' or 'moral,'" NYRW pledged. "We ask: is it good for women or bad for women?" Judged by this exacting standard, beauty contests were found wanting. They demeaned women—all women, everywhere—by depicting them as sexual playthings and commercial come-ons for the use and profit of men. What's more, by promoting artificial and demanding standards of appearance, they encouraged an entire sex to squander their lives on an obsessive, narcissistic inspection of their breasts, their thighs, their weight, their hair. But the perplexity of beauty lies in its doubleness. If beauty is oppressive, it can also provide access to pleasure, power and wealth. As long as women get extra points for fussing over their looks, then beauty can serve as an instrument of ambition.

"The curve is more powerful than the sword," Mae West once quipped, as she stroked her own luscious flanks. But beauty, like a blade, is sharp and double-edged.

*Alicia Machado of Venezuela was a slip of a thing when she took the Miss Universe title for 1996. But relaxing from a grueling regime of training and dieting, she reached for all her favorite foods after her victory. The extra pounds she gained made her the darling of the Miss Universe publicity machine, which whipped up a fake controversy about her supposed "weight problem."* AP / Wide World Photos

# Notes

p. viii    Jay Livingston and Raymond B. Evans, "French Heels," Jay Livingston Music.

p. x–xi    Mae West, as quoted by Andrea Stuart, *Showgirls,* p. 199.

p. 1    "Kid-around person" and "extra sweet," Judi Ford, as quoted by Frank Deford, *There She Is: The Life and Times of Miss America,* p. 280.

p. 2    C. A. Clarke, "What Is Beauty Anyway?" *Matrix* (July 1983): p. 9.
"Chicks to volunteer," as quoted by Robin Morgan, *Going Too Far: The Personal Chronicle of a Feminist,* p. 66.
Stokely Carmichael, as quoted by Lindsay Van Gelder, "The Truth about Bra-Burners," *Ms.,* September–October 1992, p. 80.
*Time* magazine, as quoted by Jane Stern and Michael Stern, *Sixties People,* p. 179.
Women's Liberation manifesto, as quoted by Robin Morgan, *Sisterhood Is Powerful: An Anthology of Writings from the Women's Liberation Movement,* p. xxviii.
Shulamith Firestone, as quoted by Alice Echols, *Daring to Be Bad: Radical Feminism in America, 1967–1975,* p. 56.

p. 3    "Don't Cry" slogan, as quoted by Echols, *Daring to Be Bad,* p. 57.
On Miss America, Robin Morgan, *Going Too Far,* p. 64, and *Sisterhood Is Powerful,* p. 522.

p. 5    Women's Liberation manifesto, as quoted by Robin Morgan, *Sisterhood Is Powerful,* p. 522.

p. 6    Protest slogans, as quoted by Marcia Cohen, *The Sisterhood: The True Story of the Women Who Changed the World,* p. 150.
Girdle chant, as quoted in "Miss America Pageant Is Picketed by 100 Women," *New York Times,* 8 September 1968, p. 81.
Fun, Flo Kennedy, *Color Me Flo: My Hard Life and Good Times,* p. 62.

Press release, as quoted by Morgan, *Sisterhood Is Powerful,* p. 521.
"Noxious odor," as quoted by Echols, *Daring to Be Bad,* pp. 94–95.

p. 8    Susan Brownmiller, as quoted in "Beauty You Can Take to the Bank," *Forbes,* 18 June 1984, p. 138.
"Super tacky Atlantic City," Robin Morgan, as quoted by Vicki Gold Levi and Lee Eisenberg, *Atlantic City: 125 Years of Ocean Madness,* p. 171.
Pageant official, Albert Marks, CEO of the Miss America Pageant, as quoted by Ann-Marie Bivans, *Miss America: In Pursuit of the Crown,* p. 26.
New York Radical Women principles, as quoted by Morgan, *Sisterhood Is Powerful,* p. 520.
"Anti-womanism," Carol Hanisch, "A Critique of the Miss America Protest," *Notes from the Second Year,* p. 87.

p. 13    Barnum and modern democracy, from *The Times* (London), as quoted by Brooks McNamara, "A Congress of Wonders: The Rise and Fall of the Dime Museum," *ESQ* (Third quarter 1974): p. 219.
"Everything worth seeing" and "Handsomest Ladies," from a broadside for Barnum's American Museum, 1855.
"Seduction of her charms," Oscar Commettant, *Trois ans aux Etats-Unis,* p. 37.
"Disreputable persons," from a broadside for Barnum's American Museum, 1855.
Jean-Jacques Rousseau, as quoted by Carol Wald, *Myth America: Picturing Women, 1865–1945,* p. 140.

p. 15    "Taste for fine arts," from a broadside for Barnum's American Museum, 1855.

Louise Montague, as quoted by Orin C. King, "Season of 1882: Only Big Show Coming," *Bandwagon* (May–June 1988): p. 47.

p. 17   "Types of feminine beauty," from "New York Models As Types of Beauty," *New York Times*, rotogravure section, 13 October 1907.

p. 18   Samuel Isham, as quoted by Bailey Van Hook, *Angels of Art: Women and Art in American Society, 1876–1914*, p. 56.

p. 20   "The best set," Edward Simmons, as quoted by Van Hook, *Angels of Art*, p. 152.

Phillip Stubbes, as quoted by Malcolm Cole, *Whitelands College May Queen Festival*, p. 5.

p. 23   Monsieur de Waleffe, as quoted by Raymonde Allain, *Histoire vraie d'un prix de beauté*, p. 34.

The silliness of beauty contests, Allain, *Histoire vraie*, p. 17.

Laurel Schaefer, as quoted by Ann-Marie Bivans, *101 Secrets to Winning Beauty Pageants*, p. 9.

p. 25   "Maternal blindness," Allain, *Histoire vraie*, p. 17.

*Le malin*, Allain, *Histoire vraie*, p. 18.

p. 28   "Industrial quantities," "Preface," Allain, *Histoire vraie*, p. 12.

Obedience, Allain, *Histoire vraie*, p. 37.

Photographers as artists, as quoted by Allain, *Histoire vraie*, p. 35.

Hairstylist and *la mode française*, as quoted by Allain, *Histoire vraie*, p. 48.

Railroad spokesman, as quoted by Deford, *There She Is*, p. 115.

Parisian commerce, Allain, *Histoire vraie*, p. 48.

p. 29   On Monsieur de Walffe, Allain, *Histoire vraie*, pp. 122, 21.

"Lighted sign," Allain, *Histoire vraie*, p. 59.

Virginity, Allain, *Histoire vraie*, p. 53.

Smoking, Allain, *Histoire vraie*, p. 86.

Miss Australia and the "better type," letter dated May 3, 1956, Australian Archives, A6895/1, series N56/217.

p. 30   *The Woman Worker*, as quoted by Beth Light and Ruth Roach Pierson, *No Easy Road: Women in Canada 1920s to 1960s*, p. 98.

p. 32   "Poor man's Riviera," as quoted by Mike Filey, *I Remember Sunnyside: The Rise and Fall of a Magical Era*, n.p.

Honesty, Allain, *Histoire vraie*, p. 73.

"Horn-tooting," as quoted by Levi and Eisenberg, *Atlantic City*, p. 81.

p. 33   "Jazz babies," *Atlantic City Daily Press*, 1922, as quoted by A. R. Riverol, *Live from Atlantic City: The History of the Miss America Pageant before, after and in Spite of Television*, p. 22.

Samuel Gompers, as quoted by Levi and Eisenberg, *Atlantic City*, p. 159.

p. 35   Comments re: Dorothy Britton, from a press release.

p. 36   "The distinction of sex," Rev. Horace Bushnell, as quoted by Lois Banner, *American Beauty*, p. 227.

Alfred, Lord Tennyson, *The Princess* V (II): 437–41, as quoted by Lisa Tickner, *The Spectacle of Women: Imagery of the Suffrage Campaign, 1907–14*, p. 154.

Robert Latou Dickinson, as quoted by Paula S. Fass, *The Damned and the Beautiful: American Youth* in the 1920s, p. 76.

Young woman, as quoted by Fass, *The Damned and the Beautiful*, p. 291.

p. 37   "Close embrace," editorial, *Ladies' Home Journal*, 1921, as quoted by Paula S. Fass, *The Damned and the Beautiful: American Youth in the 1920s*, p. 22.

p. 39   "Through a telescope," unidentified chorus girl, 1924, as quoted by Lewis A. Erenberg, *Steppin' Out: New York Nightlife and the Transformation of American Culture, 1890–1930*, p. 224.

"Lively girl," unidentified working woman, as quoted by Kathy Peiss, *Cheap Amusements: Working Women and Leisure in Turn-of-the-Century New York*, p. 3.

p. 41   "100% more important," unidentified placement bureau manager, as quoted by Sharon Hartman Strom, *Beyond the Typewriter: Gender, Class, and the Origins of Modern American Office Work, 1900–1930*, p. 400.

"Lovely evening dresses," unidentified working girl, 1923, as quoted by Caroline Strange, *Toronto's Girl Problem: The Perils and Pleasures of the City, 1880–1930*, p. 182.

"No amusement," Belle Israels, as quoted by Peiss, *Cheap Amusements*, p. 61.

p. 42   "Submission," as quoted by Robert Sullivan, "Thorny," *New Republic*, 4 July 1994, p. 10.

p. 45   "The real enjoyment," student at Ohio State University, as quoted by Fass, *The Damned and the Beautiful*, p. 307.

"The vitality of young womanhood," unidentified commentator, 1922, as quoted by Fass, *The Damned and the Beautiful*, p. 291.

"Magnificent and flaming audacity," Lorine Pruette, as quoted by Elaine Showalter, *These Modern Women: Autobiographical Essays from the Twenties*, p. 10.

Ida Cox, as quoted by Daphne Duval Harrison, *Black Pearls: Blues Queens of the 1920s*, p. 111

p. 50   "Sleep and eat," unidentified working woman, as quoted by Peiss, *Cheap Amusements*, pp. 43–44.

"Honey, you make me do," lyrics from "Moonlight on the Boardwalk," as quoted by Levi and Eisenberg, *Atlantic City*, p. 25.

p. 51   "Travel on wheels," unidentified young woman, as quoted by Lee Hall, *Common Threads: A Parade of American Clothing*, p. 216.

Louise Rosine, as quoted in "Bather Goes to Jail; Keeps Her Knees Bare," *New York Times*, 4 September 1921, p. 4.

p. 52   Skipping rhyme collected in Regina, Saskatchewan, as quoted by Light and Pierson, *No Easy Road*, p. 53.

p. 54   "Modern women," Phyllis Blanchard and Carlyn Manasses, as quoted by Fass, *The Damned and the Beautiful*, p. 74.

*Vogue*, as quoted by Christina Probert, *Swimwear in Vogue Since 1910*, pp. 8, 16.

p. 57    Clara Bow, as quoted by David Stenn, *Clara Bow: Runnin' Wild*, p. 12.

p. 59    Lorine Pruette, as quoted by Showalter, *These Modern Women*, p. 14.

Joan Blondell, as quoted by Deford, *There She Is*, p. 125.

"Beauty-contest mad," Harold Hall, "Why Beauty Winners Fail in the Movies," *Motion Picture*, April 1927, p. 32.

p. 60    Allain, *Histoire vraie*, pp. 90, 58, 44, 172, 173.

*The Woman Worker*, as quoted by Light and Pierson, *No Easy Road*, p. 98.

p. 61    "Lovely and unspoiled daughter," as quoted by Deford, *There She Is*, p. 131.

"Artistic and refined," Frederick Hickman, President, Atlantic City Chamber of Commerce, 1926, as quoted by Angela Saulino Osborne, *Miss America: The Dream Lives On*, p. 65.

"Epidemic," Julian Hillman and associate, Atlantic City Hotel Men's Association, as quoted by Deford, *There She Is*, pp. 129, 130.

p. 62    "Handsome in her way," "Flushing Beauty Contest Ends When Negro Girl, D. Derrick, Gains 3rd Place," *New York Times*, 21 April 1924, p. 18.

"China's Perfect Girl," as quoted by Wald, *Myth America*, p. 87.

p. 63    "Moral and mental destruction," YWCA spokesperson, as quoted in "YWCA Opens War on Beauty Contest," *New York Times*, 18 April 1924, p. 21.

Dr. Lake, as quoted by Osborne, *Miss America*, p. 76.

Max Factor, Jr., as quoted in a press release.

p. 65    Alexander Black, *Miss America*, 1887, unpaginated.

p. 66    "Worn out and useless," Atlantic City Hotel Men's Association, as quoted by Deford, *There She Is*, p. 129.

Mae West, *The Wicked Age, or The Contest*, Library of Congress Ac 16,215, 1927.

"I wrote the story," Mae West, as quoted by Andrea Stuart, *Showgirls*, p. 199

p. 69    "Iridescent bubble," *New York Times*, as quoted by Levi and Eisenberg, *Atlantic City*, p. 185.

p. 70    "Striking change," Frederick Lewis Allen, as quoted by Susan Ware, *Holding Their Own: American Women in the 1930s*, p. xvii.

"Cinderella legend," Margaret Thorp, *America at the Movies*, p. 101.

p. 71    Hobo women, Bertha Thompson with Ben Reitman, as quoted by Ware, *Holding Their Own*, p. 34.

Unidentified movie fans, as quoted by Ware, *Holding Their Own*, p. 179.

p. 72    "Miss Shearer likes," from "The Story of Norma Shearer, Hollywood's Richest Star," *Look*, 12 October 1937, p. 43.

p. 73    "The type of picture," unidentified movie producer, as quoted by Margaret Thorp, *America at the Movies*, p. 5.

Mae West, as quoted by Ware, *Holding Their Own*, p. 183.

"Seekers," Thorp, *America at the Movies*, pp. 103–4.

p. 74    Levi and Eisenberg, *Atlantic City*, p. 133.

p. 76    "Better ways," Thorp, *America at the Movies*, p. 5.

Venus Ramey, as quoted by Gerald Early, "Waiting for Miss America, *Antioch Review* 42 (Summer 1984): pp. 298–99.

p. 79    John Robert Powers, as quoted by Michael Gross, *Model: The Ugly Business of Beautiful Women*, p. 36.

Contest, Lenora Slaughter, as quoted by Osborne, *Miss America*, p. 86.

p. 81    Honor, Lenora Slaughter, as quoted by Osborne, *Miss America*, p. 86.

Jaycees, Lenora Slaughter, as quoted by Deford, *There She Is*, p. 154.

Trouble with artists, Lenora Slaughter, as quoted by Deford, *There She Is*, p. 63.

p. 83    Lotta Dempsey and Canadian Directorate of Army Recruiting, as quoted by Ruth Roach Pierson, *"They're Still Women after All": The Second World War and Canadian Womanhood*, p. 131.

Pearl S. Buck, as quoted by Susan M. Hartmann, "Prescriptions for Penelope: Literature on Women's Obligations to Returning World War II Veterans," *Women's Studies* 5 (1978): p. 235.

p. 84    Canadian Department of Munitions and Supply publicity, as quoted by Pierson, *"They're Still Women after All,"* p. 151.

Palmolive ad, as quoted by Pierson, *"They're Still Women after All,"* p. 154.

Funny thought, Thelma LeCocq, as quoted by Pierson, *"They're Still Women after All,"* p. 164.

"Morale value," from a press release.

p. 86    Advice from British women's magazines, as quoted by Jane Waller and Michael Vaughan-Rees, *Women in Wartime: The Role of Women's Magazines, 1939–1945*, pp. 80, 81.

Canadian Women's Army Corps newsletter, as quoted by Pierson, *"They're Still Women after All,"* p. 147.

Auflag 64, "Prisoners Stage Beauty Contest," *New York Times*, 9 November 1944, p. 13.

p. 87    Jean Bartel, as quoted by Deford, *There She Is*, p. 157–58.

On Jean Bartel, Lenora Slaughter, as quoted by Deford, *There She Is*, p. 158.

"Ugly little girl," Lenora Slaughter, as quoted by Deford, *There She Is*, p. 159.

"Beautiful but dumb," as quoted by Seymour Peck, "Bathing Beauty Bares Brains," unidentified New York paper, 12 September 1946.

p. 89    Raising scholarships, Lenora Slaughter, as quoted by Osborne, *Miss America*, p. 90.

Diane Sawyer, as quoted in "Crowning Moments," *People Weekly*, 15 September 1986, p. 83.

p. 92    How to Win a Beauty Contest, from Jacque Mercer, *How to Win a Beauty Contest*, pp. 79, 80, 136; Marie Leazer Farris and Verna Meer Slade, *The Beauty Pageant Manual*, p. 36; Ann-Marie Bivans, *101 Secrets to Winning Beauty Pageants*, pp. 150–51.

p. 93    Marguerite Dodd, *America's Homemaking Book,* p. 155.

p. 94    Advertising copy, as quoted by Stuart Ewen, *Captains of Consciousness: Advertising and the Social Roots of the Consumer Culture,* p. 182.

p. 97    "No, no, no," Kay D'Amico, as quoted by Brett Harvey, *The Fifties: A Women's Oral History,* p. 8.
Bess Myerson, as quoted by Susan Dworkin, *Miss America, 1945: Bess Myerson's Own Story,* p. 171.

p. 99    Dr. C. C. Crawford, *Glorify Yourself: The New Fascinating Guide to Charm and Beauty,* p. 9.
"60 Easy Ways, etc.," *Glorify Yourself: The New Fascinating Guide to Charm and Beauty,* lesson 1, cover.
"The person [she wanted] to be," Eleanor King, *Glorify Yourself: The New Fascinating Guide to Charm and Beauty,* lesson 1, p. 16.

p. 100    "Poise, dress-sense, make-up," Eric Morley, *The 'Miss World' Story,* p. 45.
Gloria Steinem, as quoted by Stuart, *Showgirls,* p. 49.
Lesley Langley, as quoted in "Miss World Stays British," *New York Times,* 20 November 1965, p. 6.
Fifties winner Neva Langley, as quoted by Bivans, *Miss America,* p. 25.

p. 103    "Reputation and stability" and "ideal American girl," "Miss America Pageant 1960 Royal Reunion Program," p. 1.
Bess Myerson, as quoted by Susan Dworkin, *Miss America, 1945: Bess Myerson's Own Story,* pp. 183, 196.

p. 104    Rule Seven, as quoted by Osborne, *Miss America,* p. 100.
"Positive protest," J. Morris Anderson, as quoted in "Miss America Pageant Is Picketed by 100 Women," *New York Times,* 8 September 1968, p. 81.

p. 105    *Ebony* magazine, as quoted by Natasha Barnes, "Face of the Nation: Race, Nationalisms and Identities in Jamaican Beauty Contests," *Massachusetts Review* (autumn 1994): p. 477.
Re Miss Black America, "Miss America Pageant Is Picketed by 100 Women," *New York Times,* 18 September 1968, p. 81.
"National problem," Lenora Slaughter, as quoted in "Miss America Aide Avoids Rights Issue," *New York Times,* 14 September 1965, p. 23.

p. 108    Dr. Zelma George, as quoted in "Beauty, She Insists, Isn't Skin Deep," *New York Times,* 8 September 1969, p. 46.
Yolande Betbeze, as quoted by Osborne, *Miss America,* p. 101.
On Yolande Betbeze, Lenora Slaughter, as quoted by Deford, *There She Is,* p. 180.

p. 109    Miss Universe director, as quoted in "Catholic Girl Heeds Church Ban, Quits Miss Universe Competition," *New York Times,* 19 July 1959, p. 46.
Mrs. Edward Belitz, "Catholic Girl Heeds Church Ban, Quits Miss America Competition," *New York Times,* 19 July 1959, p. 46.

p. 110    Hugh Hefner, as quoted by John D'Emilio and Estelle B. Freedman, *Intimate Matters: A History of Sexuality in America,* p. 302.
Exploitation, Mae West, *The Wicked Age, or The Contest,* Library of Congress Ac 16,215, 1927.
Being smart, Mae West, from "She Done Him Wrong," 1933, as quoted by Stuart, *Showgirls,* p. 195.

p. 111    Robin Morgan, as quoted in "Miss America Pageant Is Picketed by 100 Women," *New York Times,* 18 September 1968, p. 81.
Vanessa Williams, as quoted by Marcia Froelke Coburn, "The Vanessa Williams Nobody Knows," *Redbook,* March 1997, p. 78.

p. 113    Richard Nixon, as quoted by Bivans, *Miss America,* p. 5.
Seventies queen, Laurel Schaefer, as quoted by Bivans, *Miss America,* p. 26.

p. 114    "New me," unidentified woman, as quoted by William H. Chafe, *The Paradox of Change: American Women in the 20th Century,* p. 234.
Michael Grade, London *Times,* 17 November 1984, p.3.

p. 115    Margaret Gorman, as quoted by Deford, *There She Is,* p. 5.
"Sex O'Clock in America," as quoted by D'Emilio and Freedman, *Intimate Matters,* p. 233.
Palisades Amusement Park, from a press release.

p. 116    Ann Simonton, as quoted by Dana Rubin, "The Anti-Pageant," *San Jose Mercury News,* 24 June 1985, p. 2A.

p. 117    AIDS, Leanza Cornett, as quoted by Osborne, *Miss America,* p. 190.
Ducks, Leanza Cornett, as quoted in "Miss America, Can Anybody Update This Sweepstakes of Pretty?" *Glamour,* April 1994, p. 275.
Michelle Anderson, as quoted in "Miss America, Can Anybody Update This Sweepstakes of Pretty?" *Glamour,* April 1994, pp. 275–76.

p. 118    New York Radical Women principles, as quoted by Robin Morgan, *Sisterhood Is Powerful,* p. 520.
Laurie Fierstein, as quoted by Alisa Solomon, "Muscle As Art," *The Village Voice,* 9 November 1993, p. 97.

# Sources

Because of the wealth of printed, photographic and video materials that relate to beauty contests, this listing is necessarily selective. Items marked with an asterisk are recommended for further reading.

## General

Allain, Raymonde. *Histoire vraie d'un prix de beauté.* Paris: Librarie Gallimard, 1933.

*Banner, Lois W. *American Beauty.* New York: Alfred A. Knopf, 1983.

*Deford, Frank. *There She Is: The Life and Times of Miss America.* New York: Viking, 1971.

Indexes to the *New York Times* and London *Times*, 1900 to 1995.

Levi, Vicky Gold, and Lee Eisenberg. *Atlantic City: 125 Years of Ocean Madness.* Berkeley: Ten Speed Press, 1979.

*Osborne, Angela Saulino. *Miss America: The Dream Lives On.* Dallas: Taylor, 1995.

## Theory

Bordo, Susan. "Reading the Slender Body." In *Gender / Body / Knowledge: Feminist Reconstructions of Being and Knowing*, edited by Alison Jaggar and Susan Bordo, pp. 83–112. London: Rutgers University Press, 1989.

Butler, Judith. "Imitation and Gender Insubordination." In *Inside / Out: Lesbian Theories, Gay Theories*, edited by Diana Fuss, pp. 13–31. New York: Routledge, 1991.

Coward, Rosalind. *Female Desire: Women's Sexuality Today.* London: Paladin, 1984.

Cowie, Elizabeth. "Woman As Sign." In *The Woman in Question*, edited by Parveen Adams and Elizabeth Cowie, pp. 117–33. Cambridge, MA: MIT Press, 1990.

Davis, Kathy. "Remaking the She-Devil: A Critical Look at Feminist Approaches to Beauty." *Hypatia* 6, no. 2 (1991): pp. 21–43.

de Certeau, Michel. *The Practice of Everyday Life.* Berkeley: University of California Press, 1984.

Fiske, John. *Understanding Popular Culture.* Boston: Unwin Hyman, 1989.

Flax, Jane. *Thinking Fragments: Psychoanalysis, Feminism, and Postmodernism in the Contemporary West.* Berkeley: University of California Press, 1990.

Gatens, Moira. "Towards a Feminist Philosophy of the Body." In *Crossing Boundaries: Feminisms and the Critique of Knowledges*, edited by Barbara Caine, E. A. Grosz, and Marie de Lepervanche, pp. 59–70. Sydney: Allen and Unwin, 1988.

Kidwell, Claudia Brush, and Valerie Steele. *Men and Women: Dressing the Part.* Washington: Smithsonian Institution, 1989.

Kuhn, Annette. *The Power of the Image: Essays on Representation and Sexuality.* London: Routledge and Kegan Paul, 1985.

Marwick, Arthur. *Beauty in History: Society, Politics and Personal Appearance c.1500 to the Present.* London: Thames and Hudson, 1988.

Mirzoeff, Nicholas. *Bodyscape: Art, Modernity and the Ideal Figure.* London: Routledge, 1995.

Moore, Sally F., and Barbara G. Myerhoff, eds. *Secular Ritual.* Amsterdam: Van Gorcum, Assen, 1977.

Neuman, Shirley, and Glennis Stephenson, eds. *Reimagining Women: Representations of Women in Culture.* Toronto: University of Toronto Press, 1993.

Nichter, Mark, and Mimi Nichter. "Hype and Weight." *Medical Anthropology* 13 (1991): pp. 249–84.

Ortner, Sherry B. "Gender Hegemonies." *Cultural Critique* 14 (Winter 1989–90): pp. 35–80.

Rubinstein, Ruth P. *Dress Codes: Meanings and Messages in American Culture.* Boulder: Westview, 1995.

Silverstein, Brett, et al. "The Role of the Mass Media in Promoting a Thin Standard of Bodily Attractiveness for Women." *Sex Roles* 14, nos. 9/10 (1986): pp. 519–32.

Suleiman, Susan. *The Female Body in Western Culture.* Cambridge, MA: Harvard University Press, 1986.

Yuval-Davis, Nina, and Floya Anthias, eds. *Woman-Nation-State.* New York: St. Martin's Press, 1989.

## *Miss Steak*

"Beauty You Can Take to the Bank." *Forbes,* 18 June 1984, pp. 136–39.

Clarke, D.A. "What Is Beauty Anyway?" *Matrix,* July 1983, p. 9ff.

Cohen, Marcia. *The Sisterhood: The True Story of the Women Who Changed the World.* New York: Simon and Schuster, 1988.

Densmore, Dana. "On the Temptation to Be a Beautiful Object." In *Female Liberation: History and Current Politics,* ed. Roberta Salper, pp. 203–8. New York: Alfred A. Knopf, 1972.

Echols, Alice. *Daring to Be Bad: Radical Feminism in America, 1967–1975.* Minneapolis: University of Minnesota Press, 1989.

Hanisch, Carol. "A Critique of the Miss America Pageant." *Notes from the Second Year: Major Writings of the Radical Feminists.* New York: New York Radical Women, 1969.

Kennedy, Flo. *Color Me Flo: My Hard Life and Good Times.* Englewood Cliffs: Prentice-Hall, 1976.

Miss America Pageant broadcast, September 1968, distributed on videotape by the Miss America Organization, Atlantic City, N.J.

"Miss America Pageant Is Picketed by 100 Women." *New York Times,* 8 September 1968, p. 81.

Morgan, Robin. *Going Too Far: The Personal Chronicle of a Feminist.* New York: Random House, 1977.

*———, ed. *Sisterhood Is Powerful: An Anthology of Writings from the Women's Liberation Movement.* New York: Vintage, 1970.

Stern, Jane, and Michael Stern. *Sixties People.* New York: Alfred A. Knopf, 1990.

Van Gelder, Lindsay. "The Truth about Bra-Burners." *Ms.,* September–October 1992, pp. 80–81.

## *Heavy the Head That Wears the Crown*

Barnum's American Museum broadside, week of September 18, 1855. Theater Collection—Circus Material, Volume 9, Museum of the City of New York.

Brandimarte, Cynthia A. "Immaterial Girls: Prints of Pageantry and Dance, 1900–1936." *Prints and Printmakers of Texas.* Austin: Texas State Historical Society, 1997.

Chevalier, Michael. *Society, Manners, and Politics in the United States: Letters on North America.* Edited by John William Ward. New York: Anchor, 1961.

Cole, Malcolm. *Whitelands College May Queen Festival.* London: Whitelands College, 1981.

Comettant, Oscar. *Trois ans aux Etats-Unis: Étude des moeurs et coutumes américaines.* Paris: Paguerre, 1858.

Culhane, John. *The American Circus: An Illustrated History.* New York: Henry Holt, 1990.

Hess, Thomas B., and Linda Nochlin. *Woman As Sex Object: Studies in Erotic Art, 1730–1970.* London: Allen Lane, 1973.

King, Orin C. "Season of 1882: Only Big Show Coming." *Bandwagon,* May–June 1988, pp. 38, 45–47.

McNamara, Brooks. "A Congress of Wonders: The Rise and Fall of the Dime Museum." *ESQ* 20 (Third Quarter, 1974): pp. 216–34.

"New York Models As Types of Beauty." *New York Times,* rotogravure section, 13 October 1907, p. 1.

Pomeroy, Sarah B. *Goddesses, Whores, Wives, and Slaves: Women in Classical Antiquity.* New York: Schocken Books, 1975.

Ségalen, Martine, and Josselyne Chamarat. "La Rosière et la 'Miss': Les 'Reines' des fêtes populaires." *L'Histoire* 53, February 1983, pp. 44–55.

Van Hook, Bailey. *Angels of Art: Women and Art in American Society, 1876–1914.* University Park, PA: University of Pennsylvania Press, 1996.

*Warner, Marina. *Monuments and Maidens: The Allegory of the Female Form.* London: Vintage, 1996 (1985).

Wald, Carol. *Myth America: Picturing Women, 1865–1945.* New York: Pantheon, 1975.

## *Voilà, You Are Famous*

Bivans, Ann-Marie. *101 Secrets to Winning Beauty Contests.* Secaucus, NJ: Citadel, 1995.

Filey, Mike. *I Remember Sunnyside: The Rise and Fall of a Magical Era.* Toronto: Brownstone, 1981.

Light, Beth, and Ruth Roach Pierson. *No Easy Road: Women in Canada, 1920s to 1960s.* Toronto: New Hogtown Press, 1990.

"'Queen' Renounces Throne. Koran Prevents Reign of Tunis Girl Chosen as Queen of Beauty." *New York Times,* 24 January 1925, p. 13.

Riverol, A. R. *Live from Atlantic City: The History of the Miss America Pageant before, after and in Spite of Television.* Bowling Green, OH: Bowling Green State University Popular Press, 1992.

Rockwell, Norman. *Norman Rockwell: My Adventures As an Illustrator.* Garden City, NY: Doubleday, 1960.

"The World's Beauty: A Challenge." *The Lone Hand,* 1 November 1907, pp. 12–15; 2 December 1907, pp. 144, 147; 1 January 1908, p. 254; 1 February 1908, p. 364; 1 May 1908, p. 48; 1 September 1908, p. 558; 1 October 1908, pp. 628–34; 1 February 1909, pp. 410–13.

## Sex and the Single Flapper

Bland, Lucy. *Banishing the Beast: Sexuality and the Early Feminists.* New York: New Press, 1995.

Chauncey, George. *Gay New York: Gender, Urban Culture, and the Making of the Gay Male World, 1890–1940.* New York: Basic Books, 1994.

Erenberg, Lewis A. *Steppin' Out: New York Nightlife and the Transformation of American Culture, 1890–1930.* Chicago: University of Chicago Press, 1981.

*Fass, Paula S. *The Damned and the Beautiful: American Youth in the 1920s.* New York: Oxford University Press, 1977.

Hale, Nathan G., Jr. *Freud and the Americans: The Beginnings of Psychoanalysis in the United States, 1876–1917.* New York: Oxford University Press, 1971.

Harrison, Daphne Duval. *Black Pearls: Blues Queens of the 1920s.* New Brunswick: Rutgers University Press, 1988.

Higham, John. *Writing American History: Essays on Modern Scholarship.* Bloomington: University of Indiana Press, 1970.

Horn, Pamela. *Women in the 1920s.* Far Thrupp: Alan Sutton, 1995.

Laqueur, Thomas. *Making Sex: Body and Gender from the Greeks to Freud.* Cambridge, MA: Harvard University Press, 1990.

*Peiss, Kathy. *Cheap Amusements: Working Women and Leisure in Turn-of-the-Century New York.* Philadelphia: Temple University Press, 1986.

Poovey, Mary. "Speaking of the Body: Mid-Victorian Constructions of Female Desire." In *Body/Politics: Women and the Discourses of Science,* edited by Mary Jacobs, Evelyn Fox Keller and Sally Shuttleworth, pp. 29–46. New York: Routledge, 1990.

Showalter, Elaine, ed. *These Modern Women: Autobiographical Essays from the Twenties.* Old Westbury, NY: Feminist Press, 1978.

Staiger, Janet. *Bad Women: Regulating Sexuality in Early American Cinema.* Minneapolis: University of Minnesota Press, 1995.

*Strange, Caroline. *Toronto's Girl Problem: The Perils and Pleasures of the City, 1880–1930.* Toronto: University of Toronto Press, 1995.

Strom, Sharon Hartman. *Beyond the Typewriter: Gender, Class, and the Origins of Modern American Office Work, 1900–1930.* Urbana: University of Illinois Press, 1992.

Sullivan, Robert. "Thorny." *New Republic,* 4 July 1994, pp. 9–10.

Tickner, Lisa. *The Spectacle of Women: Imagery of the Suffrage Campaign, 1907–14.* Chicago: University of Chicago Press, 1988.

Woodward, Helen. *Through Many Windows.* New York: Garland, 1986 [1926].

## Sand, Surf and Stardust

Banner, Lois W. "Bow, Clara Gordon." In *Notable America Women: The Modern Period,* edited by Barbara Sicherman et al., pp. 95–97. Cambridge, MA: Belknap, 1980.

"Bather Goes to Jail; Keeps Her Knees Bare." *New York Times,* 4 September 1921, p. 4.

Fass, Paula S. *The Damned and the Beautiful: American Youth in the 1920s.* New York: Oxford University Press, 1977.

Guttmann, Allen. *Women's Sports: A History.* New York: Columbia University Press, 1991.

Hall, Lee. *Common Threads: A Parade of American Clothing.* Boston: Little, Brown, 1992.

Kasson, John F. *Amusing the Million: Coney Island at the Turn of the Century.* New York: Hill and Wang, 1978.

Light, Beth, and Ruth Roach Pierson. *No Easy Road: Women in Canada, 1920s to 1960s.* Toronto: New Hogtown Press, 1990.

Lothrop, Gloria Ricci. "A Trio of Mermaids: Their Impact upon the Southern California Sportswear Industry." *Journal of the West* 25 (1986): pp. 73–82.

Martin, Richard, and Harold Koda. *Splash! A History of Swimwear.* New York: Rizzoli, 1990.

Peiss, Kathy. *Cheap Amusements: Working Women and Leisure in Turn-of-the-Century New York.* Philadelphia: Temple University Press, 1986.

Probert, Christina. *Swimwear in Vogue Since 1910.* New York: Abbeville, 1981.

Stenn, David. *Clara Bow: Runnin' Wild.* New York: Doubleday, 1988.

## The Wicked Age

"Backers of Pageant to Sue for $2,000,000." *New York Times,* 28 November 1925, p. 17.

"Beauty Contest on Again. Merchants Take It up When Social Leaders Drop It—Negress Second." *New York Times,* 6 April 1925, p. 25.

Black, Alexander. *Miss America,* n.p., 1893.

Gilman, Sander L. *Difference and Pathology: Stereotypes of Sexuality, Race, and Madness.* Ithaca: Cornell University Press, 1985.

Gossett, Thomas F. *Race: The History of An Idea in America.* Dallas: Southern Methodist University Press, 1975.

Hall, Harold. "Why Beauty Winners Fail in the Movies." *Motion Picture,* April 1927, pp. 32–33, 114.

Hamilton, Mary Beth. *The Queen of Camp: Mae West, Sex, and Popular Culture.* London: HarperCollins, 1995.

Light, Beth, and Ruth Roach Pierson. *No Easy Road: Women in Canada, 1920s to 1960s.* Toronto: New Hogtown Press, 1990.

"Negress in 3rd Place, Beauty Contest Is Off." *New York Times,* 5 April 1924, p. 18.

Showalter, Elaine, ed. *These Modern Women: Autobiographical Essays from the Twenties.* Old Westbury, NY: Feminist Press, 1978.

Stuart, Andrea. *Showgirls.* London: Jonathan Cape, 1996.

Todd, Jan. "Bernarr Macfadden: Reformer of Feminine Form." *Journal of Sport History* 14 (Spring 1987): pp. 61–75.

Wald, Carol. *Myth America: Picturing Women, 1865–1945.* New York: Pantheon, 1975.

West, Mae. *The Wicked Age, Or The Contest.* Library of Congress Ac 16215, 1927.

"Women Condemn Beauty Parades." *New York Times*, 6 May 1924, p. 16.

"YWCA Opens War on Beauty Contest; Calls Atlantic City Parade Peril to Girls." *New York Times*, 18 April 1924, p. 21.

### Daydream Believers

"Bathing Beauties in Row. Charges That Miami Winners Were Illegally Entered." *New York Times*, 23 June 1930, p. 12.

"Combat Beauty Contests. Women Tell League Committee They Involve Moral Dangers." *New York Times*, 22 April 1931, p. 13.

Early, Gerald. "Waiting for Miss America." *Antioch Review* 42 (Summer 1984): pp. 291–305.

"New Miss America Named. Tampa Beauty Chosen at Miami When Two Are Disqualified." *New York Times*, 23 June 1930, p. 21.

"The Story of Norma Shearer, Hollywood's Richest Star." *Look,* 12 October 1937, pp. 38–43.

Thorp, Margaret. *America at the Movies.* New York: Arno Press and the New York Times, 1970 [1939].

Ware, Susan. *Holding Their Own: American Women in the 1930s.* Boston: Twayne, 1982.

### Miss America's Makeover

Anderson, Karen. *Wartime Women: Sex Roles, Family Relations, and the Status of Women during World War II.* London: Greenwood Press.

Campbell, D'Ann. *Women at War with America: Private Lives in a Patriotic Era.* Cambridge, MA: Harvard University Press, 1984.

Dennis, June. Papers (Chaperon to two Miss Canadas). Public Archives of Canada, Ottawa.

Gross, Michael. *Model: The Ugly Business of Beautiful Women.* New York: William Morrow, 1995.

Hansom, Mary Ellen. *Go! Fight! Win!: Cheerleading in American Culture.* Bowling Green, OH: Bowling Green State University Popular Press.

Hartmann, Susan M. *The Home Front and Beyond: American Women in the 1940s.* Boston, Twayne, 1982.

———. "Prescriptions for Penelope: Literature on Women's Obligations to Returning World War II Veterans." *Women's Studies* 5 (1978): pp. 223–39.

Kaledin, Eugenia. *Mothers and More: American Women in the 1950s.* Boston: Twayne, 1984.

"London Hails Beauty Queen." *New York Times*, 4 March 1943, p. 15.

Oldfield, Col. Barney. "Miss America and the 301st Bomb Group." *Air Power History* (Summer 1990): pp. 41–44.

Pierson, Ruth Roach. *"They're Still Women after All": The Second World War and Canadian Womanhood.* Toronto: McClelland & Stewart, 1986.

Prentice, Allison, et al. *Canadian Women: A History.* Toronto: Harcourt Brace, 1996.

"Prisoners Stage Beauty Contest." *New York Times*, 9 November 1944, p. 13.

Waller, Jane, and Michael Vaughan-Rees. *Women in Wartime: The Role of Women's Magazines, 1939–1945.* London: Macdonald, 1987.

"War Worker Is Voted Tanks' Miss Armorette." *New York Times*, 17 May 1943, p. 17.

Weatherford, Doris. *American Women and World War II.* New York: Facts On File, 1990.

### There She Is, Your Ideal

Bivans, Ann-Marie. *Miss America: In Pursuit of the Crown.* New York: MasterMedia, 1991.

———. *101 Secrets to Winning Beauty Pageants.* Secaucus, NJ: Citadel Press, 1995.

"Crowning Moments." *People Weekly,* 14 September 1986, p. 83.

Cumba, Ana Maria. *The World of Miss Universe.* New York: Maryland, 1975.

Dodd, Marguerite. *America's Homemaking Book.* New York: Scribners, 1957, 1968.

Dworkin, Susan. *Miss America, 1945: Bess Myerson's Own Story.* New York: Newmarket, 1987.

*Ewen, Stuart. *Captains of Consciousness: Advertising and the Social Roots of Consumer Culture.* New York: McGraw-Hill, 1977.

Farris, Marie Leazer, and Verna Meer Slade. *The Beauty Pageant Manual.* Atlanta: Pageant Manual Publishing, 1986.

*Glorify Yourself: The New Fascinating Guide to Charm and Beauty.* Marple, Cheshire: The Academy of Charm and Beauty, 1953.

Harvey, Brett. *The Fifties: A Women's Oral History.* New York: HarperPerennial, 1994.

"Judge Sees Miss World Film." London *Times*, 15 January 1966, p. 6.

Lavenda, Robert H. "Minnesota Queen Pageants: Play, Fun, and Dead Seriousness in a Festive Mode." *Journal of American Folklore* 101 (1988): pp. 168–75.

Mercer, Jacque. *How to Win a Beauty Contest.* Phoenix: Curran, 1960.

Miss America Pageant broadcast, September 1961, distributed on videotape by the Miss America Organization, Atlantic City, NJ.

"Miss World Stays British." *New York Times,* 20 November 1965, p. 6.

Morley, Eric. *The 'Miss World' Story.* n.p.: Angley Books, 1967.

Osborne, Angela Saulino. *Miss America: The Dream Lives On.* Dallas: Taylor, 1995.

Ostry, Sylvia. *The Female Worker in Canada.* Ottawa: Dominion Bureau of Statistics, 1968.

Short, Don. *Miss World: The Naked Truth.* London: Everest, 1976.

Stern, Stephen. "Ceremonies of 'Civil Judaism' among Sephardic Jews of Los Angeles." *Western Folklore* 47 (April 1988): pp. 103–28.

Strong-Boag, Veronica. "Canada's Wage-Earning Wives and the Construction of the Middle Class, 1945–60." *Journal of Canadian Studies,* no. 3 (1994): pp. 5–25.

Stuart, Andrea. *Showgirls.* London: Jonathan Cape, 1996.

## Black and White

Barnes, Natasha B. "Face of the Nation: Race, Nationalisms and Identities in Jamaican Beauty Pageants." *Massachusetts Review* (autumn–winter, 1994): pp. 471–92.

"Beauty, She Insists, Isn't Skin Deep." *New York Times*, 8 September 1969, p. 46.

"Catholic Girl Heeds Church Ban, Quits Miss America Competition." *New York Times*, 19 July 1959, p. 46.

Coburn, Marcia Froelke. "The Vanessa Williams Nobody Knows." *Redbook*, March 1997, pp. 76–79, 122, 126.

*D'Emilio, John, and Estelle B. Freedman. *Intimate Matters: A History of Sexuality in America.* New York: Harper and Row, 1988.

Dworkin, Susan. *Miss America, 1945: Bess Myerson's Own Story.* New York: Newmarket, 1987.

Early, Gerald. "Waiting for Miss America." *Antioch Review* 42 (Summer 1984): pp. 291–305.

Jewell, K. Sue. *From Mammy to Miss America and Beyond: Cultural Images and the Shaping of US Social Policy.* London: Routledge, 1993.

Keller, Bill. "Apartheid's End Transforms Beauty Show." *New York Times*, 16 September 1993, p. A1.

Levin, Elaine S. "Pageantgate Controversy Wears On." *Clearwater Sun*, 8 September 1984, from the pamphlet files at the Atlantic City Free Public Library.

Linden-Ward, Blanche, and Carol Hurd Green. *Changing the Future: American Women in the 1960s.* Boston: Twayne, 1993.

"Miss America Aide Avoids Rights Issue." *New York Times*, 14 September 1965, p. 23.

"Miss America Pageant Is Picketed by 100 Women." *New York Times*, 8 September 1968, p. 81.

"Miss America Pageant 1960 Royal Reunion Program," Atlantic City, NJ: Miss America Pageant, 1960.

Nicola-McLaughlin, Andrée. "White Power, Black Despair: Vanessa Williams in Babylon." *The Black Scholar* (March/April 1985): pp. 32–39.

Norville, Deborah. "Vanessa Williams' Extraordinary Comeback." *McCall's*, April 1992, pp. 100, 102–3, 142, 144.

Stuart, Andrea. *Showgirls.* London: Jonathan Cape, 1996.

West, Mae. *The Wicked Age, Or The Contest.* Library of Congress Ac 16215, 1927.

## The Show Must Go On

"Beauty You Can Take to the Bank." *Forbes* 133, 18 June 1984, pp. 136–39.

Bivans, Ann-Marie. *Miss America: In Pursuit of the Crown.* New York: MasterMedia, 1991.

Blank, Jonah. "The Body As Temple, the Body As Prison." *U.S. News & World Report*, 9 December 1996, p. 84.

*Chafe, William H. *The Paradox of Change: American Women in the 20th Century.* New York: Oxford University Press, 1991.

*Cohen, Colleen Ballerino, Richard Wilk, and Beverly Stoeltje. *Beauty Queens on the Global Stage: Gender, Contests, and Power.* New York: Routledge, 1996.

Crosette, Barbara. "An India Less Than Congenial." *New York Times*, 24 November 1996, section 4, p. 6.

D'Emilio, John, and Estelle B. Freedman. *Intimate Matters: A History of Sexuality in America.* New York: Harper and Row, 1988.

Drinkwater, Ros. "The Ugly Face: Why Did the Soviet Union Decide to Enter the Beauty Queen Business?" London *Times*, 4 September 1989, p. 4.

Goldman, William. *Hype and Glory.* New York: Villard, 1990.

Hamermesh, Daniel S., and Jeff E. Biddle. "Beauty and the Labor Market." *American Economic Review* 84, no. 5 (1994): pp. 1174–94.

Hulan, Leah. *Pain behind the Smile: My Battle with Bulimia.* Nashville: Eggman, 1995.

"Miss America, Can Anybody Update This Sweepstakes of Pretty?" *Glamour*, April 1994, pp. 235–37, 275–76, 281.

Morgan, Robin, ed. *Sisterhood Is Powerful: An Anthology of Writings from the Women's Liberation Movement.* New York: Vintage, 1970.

"Oh Oh, Ho Chi Minh." *Economist*, 20 May 1989, p. 46.

Rabin, Dana. "The Anti-Pageant." *San Jose Mercury News*, 24 June 1985, p. 2A.

Schillinger, Liesel. "Miss Ghana." *New Republic*, 8 and 15 January 1996, pp. 26–28.

Solomon, Alisa. "Muscle As Art." *The Village Voice*, 9 November 1993, p. 97.

Sullivan, Robert. "Thorny." *New Republic*, 4 July 1994, pp. 9–10.

Tefft, Sheila. "Good-bye Mao Cap, Hello Tiara." *Christian Science Monitor*, 12 August 1993, p. 7.

Van Esterik, Penny. "Gender and Development in Thailand: Deconstructing Display." In *Women, Feminism and Development*, edited by Huguette Dagenais and Denise Piche, pp. 264–79. Montreal: McGill-Queen's University Press, 1994.

# Index